FUMES

AND

FAITH

The Glory and Trials of
Building a Legacy From Scratch

Oz Nesbitt, Sr.

Fumes and Faith
The Glory and Trials of Building a Legacy From Scratch

Speak Up! Communications LLC
Oz Nesbitt, Sr.

Printed Worldwide
First Printing 2023
First Edition 2023

ISBN: 978-1-735-1162-3-5

10 9 8 7 6 5 4 3 2 1

Published by Gianna Brown & The Money Cheerleader LLC
Atlanta, GA Copyright 2023.

Edited by the Legacy Asset Book Academy.

An Ozism

"On life's journey,

fuming distress is a temporary precursor

to faith-bound victories

if you stay the course and remain in motion."

Table of Contents

About the Author

Born in Augusta, Georgia, Oz Nesbitt Sr. is a beacon of unwavering resolve and an exemplar of dynamic leadership. His journey from the deep-rooted Augustan soils to the bustling heart of metropolitan Atlanta propelled his evolution into a figure of prominent influence. Nesbitt's reputation as an ardent action-taker precedes him, regardless of his geographical coordinates or professional roles.

A commendable fifteen-year stint in law enforcement crystallized his historical vision and faith-laced grit. Although he laid down his police badge, he now proudly carries the mantle of an impactful government official. As a devoted public servant and astute global entrepreneur, this Commissioner, Chairman, and CEO, has been coined as a significant community staple. From rolling out college scholarships, implementing employee education programs, and promoting senior citizen benefits, his work has become his lifelong ministry. His unwavering commitment to ensuring equity is palpable, evidenced by the transformative measures he takes within his jurisdiction.

Venturing beyond public service, Nesbitt exhibits his entrepreneurial prowess with the innovative consulting firm, Speak Up! Communications, LLC. Its mission is to fuel each participant's professional growth and career development. Be it for small businesses or local schools, this firm hones both soft and hard skills for their clientele. In fostering improved workforce quality and subsequently, bolstering the welfare of various corporate structures, communities positively transform.

Affectionately known as his ride-or-die crew, his wife and four children form his steadfast backbone. He leads by example, imprinting high standards onto his lineage, his workplace, and himself. To this light, he courageously sparks tough, at times, controversial discussions, to progressively move the pendulum across diverse areas.

Whether Nesbitt finds himself at the helm of his family, a governmental institution, or an entrepreneurial venture, three cardinal principles always guide his path: attitude, approach, and appearance. He firmly believes that when these "Three A's" are backed by divine favor, they can facilitate one's journey to unbridled success. For him, a structure's strength is directly proportional to the solidity of its foundation, allowing it to weather life's tumultuous storms with grace. In his worldview, the most enduring cornerstone is Jesus Christ and His teachings. By accepting this faithful provision, Nesbitt believes anyone can emulate his legacy, living a life infused with purpose, leadership, and a ceaseless commitment to serve.

Acknowledgements

ONE MILLION THANKS to Ms. Gianna Brown and The MC Team. My overall experience has been exceptionally stress-free. The one-on-one coaching seamlessly captured the highs and lows of my life story while crafting this best-selling book. Your Legacy Asset Book Academy made my experience less intimidating, easy-to-follow and flexible. My complex schedule/calendar was embraced and managed like a well-oiled machine without "glitches". The professional editing complimented and captured my authentic personality without losing my genuine, raw character.

A SPECIAL THANK YOU and shout out to my super outstanding, talented Executive Assistant, Mrs. Andrea Lee. I could not have successfully completed this book project without your help and support. The disciplined weekly schedule you crafted incorporated my book milestones. Hence, I had designated time to focus on this project completion without distractions and interruptions.

TO SAPELO ISLAND AND THE GULLAH COMMUNITY: thank you for providing a rich escape for me to cultivate my writer's zone. From the ocean breeze to the authentic interactions, I was gifted the uninterrupted chance to reflect on my life and tune in to my ancestors.

Preface

This literary work you curiously hold is an authentic expression of how my life's story unraveled over these last fifty-plus years. As you read, the anecdotes and advice, occasionally wrapped with comical relief, are about channeling unlimited perseverance to boldly withstand the test of time. By courageously persevering over mountainous obstacles and through dubious valleys, I unmasked my innate ability to keep moving forward, from trials to glories. In massively challenging seasons, I dug deep and fought against all odds, even though my resource reservoir tanked below empty. Such pursuits were undoubtedly incredibly tasking. Nonetheless, I bravely ran on the bare minimum toward more significant outcomes, encountering a better version of myself around each curve and corner.

As a child reared in Augusta, Georgia's second-largest city, I discovered a strikingly profound and distinct fire burning at the innermost pit of my existence. I never subscribed to touted, crippling statistics. I possessed no unction to be labeled average. Being confined to a mediocre standard of living was unnerving, thus propelling me to rise above economic disparities and systemic oppression. In turn, I resolved to fortify my faith and pursuits. Gratefully, notable mentors and wise family members played a crucial role in developing my adeptness in navigating new roles in varying cities along my journey. One of my overarching goals for this written endeavor is to replicate those selfless actions, hence conveying deeper insights as to how you can also trace an ambitious path to your successful reality.

Throughout each chapter, you'll learn how I faithfully catapulted my life to the next level by leveraging my uncapped self-determination and tapping into my illustrious influencers. Over many years, operating on fumes has been synonymous with being strapped for cash or scraped to the bare bone. Not only were financial lack and emotional exhaustion at play, but I also navigated eighty percent of my adulthood without a living parent. During my most laborious seasons, I yearned for this biological connection and genuine encouragement. Painstakingly continuing my perilous path proved lonely, arduous, or sometimes profoundly scary. Dense, emotionally charged fumes clouded my mind at those inevitable intersections, choking my intellectual engine. Hence, the only way to overcome this was to lean on my immortal Father, God, activating even more profound belief. Time after time, He stepped in when I was at my wit's end, right before my brewing breakdown.

A vision-based approach is an empowering tool to change life's trajectory. Whether during my educational or professional experiences, setting my sights on a gratifying goal kept me grounded. In times of disarray and imbalance, I leaned heavily on pre-existing talents. I boldly trusted my unique skill set would pave the way to career breaks. Even with a broken spirit and hefty load, I course-corrected, shifting my overall mindset. After all, Jesus commands us to come to Him when weary and heavily burdened. That is precisely what I did. Like the Creator, I could construct an unbelievable life, starting with my imagination and decisive action. Like Japanese art, Kintsugi, I harnessed the shattered dreams of my ancestors. I picked up remarkable pieces of each person throughout my family and city. Then, with a gold-dipped, faithful aim, I molded those broken pieces into a renewed vessel of a notable life, despite extremely humble beginnings. Despite being given the short end of the resource stick, marginalized trailblazers like President Obama and inventor Lonnie Johnson soared to unfathomable heights. Thus, you can also move the barometer upward against any surmounting pressures, then put your faith-filled dreams into daily action. But first, you must see it in your mind and believe it is possible in your heart.

Via frequent conversations with my mentors and mentees, I surmise that many people endure a myriad of taxing bumps on roadways, just like me. In fact, the inquisitive person peering over your shoulder to read a snippet of this book could be drowning in a defeated pothole of pure anguish. When you address such a fiery reality, the journey becomes a smoother but equally progressive coast. Acknowledge your present circumstance, then adjust your perspective accordingly. How you experience a twenty-four-hour period is an intentional exchange of input and output. Negative thinking and scarcity mindsets only beget adverse outcomes in a vicious cycle. On the contrary, abundant thinkers who pursue goals with a positive guise will intuitively encounter more favorable results. The latter vantage point paves a more distinct, straightforward pathway lined with great expectation. Your attitude and approach will determine your aggregate altitude.

Once you have completed a mental paradigm shift, the world is your rewarding oyster, especially if you choose your circle wisely. Fear magnifies fear, just as iron sharpens iron. The company you keep correlates directly with your potential to thrive across all spectrums. The caveat is you must trust your intuition, hiring or firing people at will. Essentially, life is a personal business with no days off. Surround yourself with like-minded, goal-oriented individuals committed to progression. Such relationships, aligned with purpose-driven goals, will strategically anchor you in substance and keep your sights laser-focused on future objectives. Anyone you intentionally eject from your life's game is dead weight, only stifling your growth and choking your ambition. Do not allow anyone to place a label on you that does not highlight the immense greatness you possess as a child of the Most High. Without them, your load is lighter, and the road ahead is clearer. Choosing to co-sign a sub-par life contract or forgo a promising future is complete blasphemy.

Break away from any foreign or domestic atomic object that may be making excruciating attempts to manipulate your mind. These naysayers blindly embolden you to park permanently in a comfortable abyss of mediocrity. Even former friends or current allies may occasionally transform into your present-day haters. No worries: this nonconstructive criticism is a clear indication of your unique growth. Remember, their envy blatantly mirrors the inadequacies they attempt to project onto you as they throw frivolous obstacles along your path to success. My book sales data will soon reveal a definitive list of individuals who abhor my very existence. These prying readers continue to be engulfed in my daily affairs and accomplishments. Unfortunately for them, their hope to discover a self-inflicted confession powerful enough to dismantle my legacy is misplaced. Like the Wicked Witch of the West in *The Wizard of Oz*, these begrudging people will melt away in self-imposed misery. They will be greatly disappointed page by page, as this tangible compilation serves as a token pivot of more substantial progress.

This candid book pulls back the curtain of a county chairman to unveil an everyday down-to-earth guy loaded with uncontainable drive. The valiant ascension to noteworthy wins and eradication of generational curses is a lofty pursuit. You are engineered for this most worthwhile mission. Recast external envy. Then, repurpose internal fear into supernatural fuel that drives you forward on the success route. Whether puttering along on fumes or coasting easy with a refueled tank of faith, keep your foot on the gas. Advance with a laser-focused vengeance.

Even if no one parades around you to encourage a pending rise from your current demise, lean on God's promising forecasts. Then, tap into the god within you, dragging yourself out of a tar-laced swamp of misery. Refashion intended obstacles into advantageous opportunities. Garnered lessons from daily ebbs and flows positioned me to become a better man and leader. I willfully reframed my esteemed self-image with pillars of discipline and inspiration planted upon my house on the Rock, our God. My message is crystal clear:

There is no time, talent, or dollar to waste. Seize every moment as if it is your last chance to fulfill your greatest purpose. After all, no one is promised tomorrow.

By sharing my story against the backdrop of life's dualities, I serve as a living testament that there is a rewarding light at the end of the road. Never give up. Stay the course. On fumes and faith, through toils and snares, I've already overcome. Watch out, world; I am just warming up!

To God be the glory.

Dedication

I dedicate this first book to my lovely powerhouse, Aunt Mattie. You have always been the apple of my eye. To you, I will always extend sincere appreciation and heartfelt respect.

Throughout my most impressionable years, I witnessed your daily existence gracefully serve as a shining example of an optimistic attitude. Your classy and resilient approach to life is unmatched and admired. Living under your roof and learning your incredible story broadened my horizons, encouraging my global mission. Not only did you operate as a core resource for burgeoning leaders and aspiring college students, but you also carved out intentional time to help me navigate my personal pursuits. I am immensely grateful for every moment we shared and every lesson you ingrained in me. I credit my ambitious drive to your wise interventions and effervescent mentoring. From intentionally teaching me how to navigate robust inner circles of promising leaders, your active role cultivated my manhood and catapulted my aspirations. Even though I chose to pursue an immediate career outside the academic route you envisioned, your love and support never wavered. You were a constant presence in my ever-changing world.

It is no secret that you were the most significant person in my life. Your energy has been the wind beneath my wings, from celebratory cards to frank, insightful feedback. You are the essence of a remarkable woman. I will be eternally grateful for your influential impact on my life.

As I hold this first book, I humbly pray each chapter, recounted from a half-century of existence here on Earth, continues to make you proud. I extend immeasurable gratitude as your grace beams down on me from Heaven.

Thank you for continuing to be my ever-present, elegant guardian angel. My heart will forever save a special place for you, my first-class and cherished aunt.

Chapter 1
Matriarchs and Mothers Matter

On November 22, 1963, a vicious sniper assassinated then-President John F. Kennedy while he was riding in his presidential motorcade. As his protective wife cradled his bloodied body in her lap, the convertible rushed to Parkland Memorial Hospital, but it was too late—another president had been killed in the line of duty. The nation mourned. Such an astonishing turn of events made longtime Senator Lyndon Johnson the new chief commanding officer. Vice President Johnson delivered his magnanimous vision of building "A Great Society" for the American people, inclusive of significant welfare expansion. To restore some semblance of progressive hope, he also rolled out additional tactics within his first ninety days to combat racial inequality, staggering crime, and mounting poverty. Like Kennedy, Johnson advocated for educational programs and Medicare, both plausible, promising equalizers for building generational wealth. Johnson's legacy also echoed a ubiquitous goal to rebuild the entire urban United States over the next four decades.

Overall, the country subscribed to Johnson's vision and witnessed his steadfast fight to give citizens some measure of normalcy. Voters trusted him to champion causes that widened access to equitable opportunities outside of being drafted for global warfare. The Vietnam War commenced less than two years after President Johnson's re-election in 1964. However, this decision was met with strong opposition from heavyweight leaders, such as Muhammad Ali, who blatantly used his platform to cement his anti-war posture. For Ali, like many Americans, domestic battles against economic and educational inequities held higher importance. One sole fight worthy of nonrefundable time was one that added children to family units and dividends to bank accounts.

Just two weeks after Muhammad Ali knocked out Karl Mildenberger, the European Heavyweight Champion from Germany, three times in a single match, an additional ground-breaking event transpired in the heart of Augusta, Georgia. After a few rounds of contractions, my mother, Lillie Mae, affectionately known as Peggy, entered the maternity ward. Knee-deep in prayers, she prepared to knock out the birth of another historical figure: me. On Monday, September 26, 1966, at Piedmont August Hospital, formerly Augusta University Hospital, Peggy Nesbitt gave birth to a Generation X member, Osborn ("Oz") Nesbitt. Undoubtedly a September to remember, my mother swaddled me in a blue-striped, white cotton blanket. She then tenderly introduced me to her first-born child, Gregory. As she gazed upon my older brother and me, her initial enjoyment of family expansion was abruptly interrupted by the heightened need for a larger home. Yet, expanded square footage came with substantially higher expenses, also posing an irrefutable need for a higher income.

Since the Great Depression flooded the United States with bank foreclosures and poverty, elected officials stepped in to mitigate household dilemmas. Curtailed mortgage lending and interest rates made breadwinners depart from the refined homeownership pathway. Numerous government programs continued to be instrumental as working-class families navigated parenthood coupled with economic demands. For example, the Federal Housing Administration worked to minimize economic hurdles by creating The Housing Act of 1937. Under this new initiative, elected politicians voted to earmark a certain percentage of tax dollars for public housing, positioning families to jump over homelessness status. This funding trickled down from the White House to the corridors of low- and middle-class homes. As a result, Augusta city officials collectively agreed to construct three housing projects. The city broke ground for one of these infallible units, Sunset Homes, in 1939.

Approximately thirty years after this construction, my vibrant, hard-working mother, Peggy Nesbitt, scoured Augusta for a spacious place to raise a family. Then, she located this housing development nestled between Hunter and McCauley Streets. She applied, qualifying for accompanying government subsidies. Once she signed the rental agreement, we packed up our home located on Linden Street. In our new neighborhood, working-class families occupied every unit and worked to establish an environment of unmatched unity. From the tender age of two, I called this four-hundred-townhome real-estate village, sprinkled with courtyards, my haven.

Whether residents were jovially throwing water balloons or running from occasional downpours, we harmoniously coexisted within a community later renamed Cherry Tree Crossing. In no time, neighbors morphed into a unified village committed to the betterment of all families of Sunset Homes. This community's name was befitting given the loving childhood and overall good life we enjoyed. Our decor was comprised of plastic-covered sofas, wooden side tables, twin beds, and floor-to-ceiling lamps. Not only did our home overflow with warmth but our refrigerator and closets also provided ample storage for perfect amounts of food or clothing.

Our parental dichotomy offered a contrasting but mutually respectable dynamic. Although my mortal creators divorced, both undertook active roles in our child-rearing, especially my superwoman, Ms. Peggy. My mother was a tremendous force of nature while I was growing up. She was a brown-skinned, athletically built woman who operated as purpose-driven and real as they came. Her authentic disposition was a constant presence in her three boys' lives and displayed in her unwavering commitment to our well-being. Depending on the hour, Mom wore many hats—protector, provider, prayer warrior, or domestic manager—and approached this multifaceted responsibility with sheer determination.

Mom was the spick-and-span queen. Guests relished fresh scents of lemon Pine-Sol and bleach once they crossed the threshold into our home. Presumably, our tidy home would easily win the cleanest apartment award if such a competition ever arose. My mother subscribed to the popular belief that cleanliness was close to godliness. She included her three boys in weekly house maintenance activities, which would inevitably translate to our future ability to be responsible homeowners. When I was old enough to write my name and multiply single-digit numbers, Gregory placed a cleaning rag in my hand. By that time, our baby brother Zachary (Bar-T) was a toddler and watched us work from the sofa.

On Saturday mornings, my siblings and I were awake and working long before we could play outside. Our mom had taught us to do any assigned chores, tasks, and assignments at the crack of dawn. Restoring our place to its guest-ready state included weekly objectives, such as cleaning the floors, organizing the refrigerator, or doing the dishes. As another testament to underscore the importance of order as stated explicitly in the Bible, my churchgoing mother raised us to value orderliness, organization, and detail-oriented work.

Thankfully, her teaching taught us to take pride in our home's maintenance. Each chore was approached with purpose and determination. For instance, we discovered Pledge and a soft cloth work best for polishing wood furniture instead of dishwashing liquid or Windex. Dusting followed sweeping to ensure no leftover particles lingered. Our physical exertion also included the four-step laundry process:

1. My vibrant siblings and I separated the whites from colored items.
2. We added the first load of dyed sheets, followed by multi-colored materials.

3. We carefully added a cap full of bleach to the white load.

4. While the washer ran, we shook and hung the damp items along the clothesline in our backyard.

Believe it or not, we efficiently completed all assigned duties like a mainstream assembly line before eleven each morning because we diligently worked as a team. After Mom gave everything a second look, she smiled approvingly. Then, we eagerly jetted to the blessed outdoors at lightning speed.

My mother's demands for respecting our estate and other people's property were unequivocal. I recall going down the road with my family and coming across litter along the sidewalk. Mom's severe expression told us everything we needed to know without a single utterance. She clearly conveyed, "You'd never even consider doing that." Her words were like a mandate, permanently etched in stone into our youthful minds. I wouldn't dare forget. Such teachable moments crystallized an expectation I uphold via high civic obligations and pre-established house rules.

Ms. Peggy embodied unbound faith and tough love. As people in the neighborhood established relationships with her, Mama yielded the utmost respect from every responsible renter. Although my mother forwent her college education, her authentic communication skills were the icing on the cake. She spoke a language people from all walks of life could understand. If you needed clarification, she paused and broke down her messaging. When she finished telling you like it was, you were crystal clear. In the same light, if Mama told us something, we followed her orders to a T. Her presence commanded the attention of any room, as well as the most profound depths of all ear canals. Anyone with any sense understood that when Mama showed up, you paid attention.

As we neared the end of each month, she picked up extra hours to earn additional income. Her longtime client once requested that Mom work an early Saturday morning shift to prepare for her daughter's engagement party. Once she cooked a five-course breakfast, her tight lips communicated clear directives to us.

"Boys, I am heading to work for a few hours."

We gathered in the small foyer, then endearingly hugged her waist.

"Gregory (Greg) is in charge, but I expect you to take care of each other while I am gone. Once I lock this door, do not open it for a single soul. I mean nobody. No exceptions," she directed.

As she grabbed her purse from the coffee table, we nodded in agreement and synchronously said, "Yes, ma'am."

Between Mom's stern tone and strong presence, her crystal-clear announcement was inevitably law. She literally placed the fear of God in us, and we knew she meant business. Her commands were etched heavily into our hippocampi, like the Ten Commandments on the stone tablets. Yet, on this given Saturday, visitors coincidentally tested our ability to follow Mom's house commands. At the crack of dawn, on any given Saturday, consecutive door knocks were quite common. From neighboring churches sharing Krispy Kreme doughnuts fundraisers to Jehovah's Witnesses sharing their gospel, our ability to follow Mom's orders was tested.

Once we finished eating breakfast and cleaning the dishes, we heard a familiar knock on our door. We gazed at each other, becoming utterly mute. Shaking our heads to imply a standstill, we silently communicated a shared understanding: "Do not even think about it." We froze on the sofa momentarily before cautiously saying in unison, "Hello."

As fate would have it, our beloved Aunt Mattie paid us an impromptu visit.

"Hi, boys, it's your Aunt Mattie."

Since we were not expecting any visitors, even if it was our second mother, we remembered our directives and refused to open the door. She knocked again, but more adamantly.

Zachary and I walked over to the green government window, carefully pulling back the shade to peek outside. Sure enough, it was my mother's only sibling, Aunt Mattie.

"Hi, Aunt Mattie. Mama said we cannot open the door."

Shocked to learn neither of us would budge to grant her access, she pleaded for a few additional minutes. Then, she strolled back to her car. Although in disbelief, she chuckled at the level of unwavering respect my brothers and I illustrated for my mom, even if it meant denying our favorite aunt's entry. Being disobedient was not an option. We would not grant anybody access, even if it were Jesus and his twelve disciples who showed up at our house. They would literally have to move through the steel government door, then teleport themselves to our living room to be in our presence.

No one will ever know whether this was a premeditated test crafted by two sisters collectively raising three boys or a mere coincidence. Yet I am confident my siblings and I were unwilling to risk it all to figure out its cause. The associated consequences and stakes to unlock the door were too high, after all. Active parenting was in full swing during our upbringing. This child-rearing featured the fear of the Lord and a rod at play. Ms. Peggy never spared the rod when needed. My heart turned cold each time I heard Mom command, "Take it off," coupled with an immediate oration of our full government names. Oh, did Mama mean business! Such a direct order indicated a few licks with the leather belt were soon to follow. I did everything in my power to avoid my mother's periodic wrath. Additionally, our family bond needed to embody fundamental integrity and trust. Then, and only then, could we create a conducive safe place for Mama to work her magic in the kitchen.

Fast-food restaurants and convenience stores captured less than ten percent of my mother's hard-earned dollars, but nothing could compare to my mom's home cooking. After utilizing government assistance and Mom's disposable income, we eagerly filled our kitchen with allotted goods for the month. It was an unstated truth that we deserved to eat good and live well. Not only were Mom's superb cleaning skills visibly evident throughout our humble abode, but her cooking talents were also equally prevalent. My mother could cook; I am not referring to a simple plated rice and baked chicken meal. From my point of view, she was only, if any, shots shy of being a Michelin-star chef. Although she boasted about her culinary skills to family and friends, she could confidently reinforce her words by serving a mouth-watering dish at the drop of a dime. In fact, the holiday season nearly monopolized our kitchen activities. Neighbors and family members placed requests for festivity cakes and holiday pies. Ultimately, we ran a seasonal, home-based restaurant that generated extra income. This rush kept us busy and connected. Plus, there were the added bonuses to us boys of all the sugary goodness and licking the mixing spoons.

Holidays were a huge deal in our home as well. These annual festivities ushered in a glorious family affair. Mom went all out to make it grand. First, we outlined our front door with a gold garland and placed a Merry Christmas sign in the center. Then, we pulled our artificial Christmas tree from a storage box. After unfolding the branches, we wrapped this six-foot pine in egg-shaped lights and added dozens of golden-winged red cardinals. Its final complement was this shiny silver ornament, which made bird chirping sounds every hour. Once our tree was decorated to perfection, we unboxed the color wheel. This circular contraption operated similarly to a fan. We angled it from the floor, then marveled at the projected yellow, orange, red, and purple lights on our tree. Then, for the next couple of weeks, Ms. Peggy used the money she stashed away over the course of the year to fill up the tree parameter. My mom was intentional about gift-giving, and she often involved us in the selection process. Once the annual O'Tasco catalogue arrived in the mail, Mom would tell her three boys to each circle their top three desired items. Nine times out of ten, Mom would put her heart and soul into wrapping the exact gifts we desired with perfect bows. All the bikes were discreetly rolled in late at night on Christmas Eve.

Just a few days before Thanksgiving, each passerby caught a pleasant whiff of soul food. Our home smelled like Thanksgiving and

Christmas jubilee every night from November to New Year's Eve. Unlike my brothers, I gravitated towards the opportunity to be Mom's sous-chef by lending a helping hand. From old-school R&B to gospel beats, especially the Queen of Soul, Aretha Franklin, Mom engendered a warm, memorable occasion for all present parties. A musical backdrop crystallized our family bonds while our mother utilized the kitchen counter as her culinary canvas to craft appetizing masterpiece after masterpiece. She reigned as the queen of the kitchen on any given day. Although she worked egregiously long shifts keeping the pieces of other people's homes together, she still managed our family affairs and motherly duties superbly. Her mac-n-cheese, fried pork chops, and string beans created the most sumptuous five-star meal, bar none. Every delectable bite had Peggy's love and pride whipped up in it.

So, when organizing my tenth birthday celebration, it was no surprise I automatically designated my mom as the chief event planner. Leveraging her holiday party hits, domestic manager talents, and unconditional love for me, my party would go off without a hitch. As I unveil that joyous memory, it is as if this decadal event occurred only yesterday.

Mama asked me, "Oz, your big day is right around the corner. What do you want for your birthday?"

Smiling from ear to ear, like a kid at his favorite candy store, I replied, "I want the largest birthday party ever. I can invite my classmates and neighborhood friends. Then, we can tell the family to come over too."

Mom grinned. "You got it, son. I will make it happen."

As we lounged on the sofa, she creatively spewed out equally impressive ideas. Of course, I agreed with all her propositions. I thought, *Mom knows how to host the best parties. I know it will knock me off my feet with satisfaction.*

That momentous Saturday, my birthday celebration mirrored a July 4th community cookout. My mother laid it out in high fashion. With red, blue, and white streamers and balloons, my guests arrived with gifts and a few casserole dishes.

Hot dogs, hamburgers, potato salad, chips, cookies, and Kool-Aid: you name it, we had it, and unlimited amounts too. Aunts, uncles, grandparents, cousins, and friends sported our tri-color theme and gathered around to sing "Happy Birthday." Mom strolled out with my cake decorated with American flags. She baked the moistest, equally sweet, three-layer red, white, and blue birthday cake. While the ten candle flames flickered brightly, I basked in the gracious glory of being celebrated by those I cherished.

Existing pride in my country, community, and identity skyrocketed, exploding like gleeful fireworks. While I opened my gifts and shared my brand-new bag of green army men with my schoolmates, I experienced my nirvana. In that singular moment, I was undeniably the happiest boy in Richmond County. My September-to-remember surpassed even my wildest imagination. Nineteen-seventy-six marked one of my favorite reunions. That single day that honored my first decade on Earth left a lasting imprint on me. Now with over fifty birthdays and annual celebrations in my repertoire, my tenth birthday still reigns supreme. The way my mother made my day is permanently tattooed across my heart. As I recounted that fall weekend, I relived those joyous memories and warm, delightful emotions like it was yesterday.

Despite having young boys in a society with predetermined gender roles, Mom also instilled the values of spiritual soundness, premier cooking, and excellent housekeeping in us, which we kept well into adulthood. While the world never crowned me the most incredible cook, I ain't lost in the kitchen. My mother taught me the art of creating some exquisite culinary masterpieces, such as her legendary cornbread dressing recipe. In retrospect, each time I scrub a pot or a toilet, I realize how lucky we were to have such a phenomenal matriarch. I am eternally grateful for my mother's relentless work ethic and constant commitment. Through her tireless efforts and positive outlook, she provided us with a steady, sturdy, and decent lifestyle, regardless of our physical address, income status, or school district.

Mothers And Matriarchs Make The World Revolve

Unlike most mammals, human mothers are permanent nurturers and resources from the moment they give birth to a child to the moment they cease to exist. These stay-at-home or gainfully employed females usually have an around-the-clock commitment, working tirelessly with no days off. Unless her partner or immediate family recognizes such laborious demands put on her daily, she often must forgo paid vacation time and sick leave. Salary.com published an article in 2019 calculating the median annual salary of $162,581 to be adequate for stay-at-home caregivers given the hourly investment. To the same extent, of the 141 countries offering maternity leave, only forty-one attach a monetary stipend matching their employee salary. On a global scale, a birth-giver's value carries diverse perspectives, but I am confident every child is only here because of a mother.

While the annual celebration on the second Sunday of May is a noteworthy effort to honor these matriarchs, it only skims the surface of the deserving celebratory acts that should be awarded to the full-time role of mothering. Renaissance poet and Columbia University Graduate, Langston Hughes, captured the messages transmitted from a mother to her offspring. In his 1922 poem, "Mother to Son," Hughes uses his mother's voice to set a tone for a tumultuous but conquerable journey. In this poetic diction, the mother addresses the consistent climb that commences from birth, an ascension with hurdles, pain, and stumbles. Within this wise monologue, it is a woman's maternal instinct to place her survival and success above systemic oppression. She proudly proclaims, "Life for me ain't been no crystal stair, but I am still going, honey." By painting a realistic view of struggles and triumphs, the mother encourages the son to keep striving for excellence, just as she has. Through these verses, mothers are charged with exemplifying integrity, resilience, and vision, even when combatting painful realities.

Mothers are the true epitome of Wonder Woman. Like the Justice League co-created by this DC Comic's character, child-bearing women are a powerful force who reign as Amazonian Queens in their own right. Yet, these feminine beings can channel a warrior spirit to protect their young in the blink of an eye. In this light, my brothers and I inevitably inherited a portion of her fierce heart and tall standards. Even when up against adversity, Mom never lost faith or faltered in her resolve. By witnessing such resilient and resourceful traits, we understood that if we faced problems with grace and dignity, we would overcome them as victors.

Her legacy lives on in each of us. We fervently strive daily to make her proud. I hope she is smiling down on us from Heaven as we try our mighty best to keep her blessed memory alive every waking moment.

Chapter 2
A Legacy of Men and Mentors

Tracing generational accomplishments shows, evidently, that a predisposition for success is attached to our forefathers and foremothers. Lineage can be a glimmer of hope or a reminder of flaws. In my immediate family, Aunt Mattie was the only college graduate. She proudly waved the flag of degree attainment. I frequently admired her three degrees framed on her living room wall. Between her and my mom, my cognitive growth was a priority. Hence, I routinely did my homework after school as soon as I entered the house. It was gratifying to convey the successful completion of an assignment when questioned. After family dinner, I would cuddle up with a good book before drifting into a deep nightly slumber. These daily disciplines placed my scored oratory and literary skills in the top percentile. So, I was awestruck when I missed the mark for statewide academic standards. These newfound deficits put me in an unexpected compromising situation.

Shortly after Black History Month, my sixth-grade experience tested my remaining happiness and optimistic outlook. While Language Arts and History Studies were an attainable joy, I worked hard to keep a passing grade in Mathematics. The fast-paced math curriculum catapulted me into vastly different realms, like an exploding meteor. This task proved quite successful initially since the first units focused on simple arithmetic, fractions, and multiples. Nevertheless, before I could fully comprehend ratios, percentages, and algebraic expressions, we were shifting to a new unit on geometry, and the teachings were moving faster than Wendell Scott's first Grand National Series victory. Regrettably, I arduously fought to keep up with my classmates as they left me in the arithmetic dust.

As spring break approached, my parents confronted the harsh reality that I had not met all the required milestones to advance to the seventh grade. After discussing this reality over a friendly card game, my mom and dad agreed to a meeting with Dr. Charles L. Butler, the school's principal. At this conjecture, despite the academic plan implemented by my teachers, I failed to catch up on the math curriculum. Neither tutorials nor additional enrichment eradicated the existing gaps.

"Hello, Principal Butler. Thank you for offering the opportunity for Oz to continue to the next grade with his peers," my dad said as he greeted him with a handshake.

"Absolutely, Mr. Nesbitt. We want children to progress to the next level. Sometimes, the student avoids additional hiccups in the challenging subject. The next grade entails an initial reteaching process for their first month, which typically minimizes academic gaps," Principal Butler explained.

"Yes, I understand. However, after discussing this with my ex-wife, we decided it's best to retain him in the sixth grade," my dad recanted.

Quite shocked, Principal Butler countered, "I am curious. Most parents jump at this promotion opportunity. What was your rationale?"

"As men, we know it is vital young boys are held accountable for the results they get and learn the true essence of hard work. If we hand Oz an unearned victory, then we rob him of the chance to be victorious by his merit," my dad emphatically answered.

Like most family units, relationships are unique to encompassing personalities. Yet there are some non-negotiable standards. In my family, the pinnacle has always been a strong work ethic.

This setback underscored my leadership attributes (my three A's)—attitude, appearance, and approach— decades before I verbalized my speaking motto across global stages. From that point forward, I shifted my technique, reinforcing my self-worth. This catalytic experience fostered my "whatever it takes" disposition for conquering goals. Being blindsided by this unexpected verdict of retainment lit a burning fire within me, which only intensified with the years. Re-entering the same classrooms and halls but with a different peer group embarrassed me throughout middle school. Such a humbling experience multiplied my resilience and focus tenfold. This abrupt decision enhanced my coping skills, especially in handling startling events and disappointments more constructively.

For centuries, elders have indoctrinated children to believe fathers know best. In many regards, I agree with this line of thinking, even when the initial directive seems unfair to a novice child. Although they did not live under the same roof, my parents maintained an amicable relationship. I remember observing their card games and thinking, *"Wow, they love healthy competition."* As strong-willed as both were, they supported and further iterated the decisions each one made regarding their offspring.

As a Korean War veteran, my military dad took full advantage of his domestic time. We built an indestructible bond, even though living outside my primary residence limited our interactions. He was consistent with his duality of life: a workaholic by day and a productive alcoholic by night. Although he stood at five foot, five inches and weighed about one hundred and eighty pounds, his behavior served as a significant weekend marker. Dad, also known as Shorty, was the life of the party. He lived the work-hard, play-hard philosophy to the fullest. Whether he partook in adult libations sparingly or indulgently, I loved him immensely and always showed him the utmost respect. Now, some nights his behavior did sting my soul. My friends recounted his drunken fall to the ground when they saw me. However, I found no humor in watching my dad repeatedly inch closer to his final breath.

Even in my youth, I heard adults discuss the horrid realities of battled soldiers unable to regain their full footing as working citizens. Some men ended up homeless, jobless, and hopeless. I could not fathom the depth of my father's deeply rooted post-traumatic stress disorder (PTSD) and daily battle against ever-present racism. In the US alone, three million people are diagnosed with PTSD each year, with the stimulus being war, abuse, or traffic collisions. If I had the miracle pill to liberate these people and my father from internal pain and mental agony, I would consider it a miraculous blessing. However, instead of focusing on this far-fetched wish, I made it my duty to graduate and change the narrative for Nesbitt men.

When I matriculated at my high school, I was still profusely disturbed that my graduation year had fallen behind my closest friends. The optimal time to catch up and finish high school with my kindergarten class had arrived. Hence, I proactively scheduled an in-person meeting with my high school guidance counselor, Mr. Leroy James. After he juxtaposed my current credits with the graduation requirements, we crafted a year-round schedule to put me back on track. I could not have been more grateful to Mr. James. Instead of meddling or working each summer, I enrolled in a few courses. Whether it rained or shined, I moved hell and high water to get to my classes before the bell rang. I ran, walked, or rode my ten-speed bike to the school, depending on my departure time. If the weather forecast predicted torrential rains or storms, Aunt Mattie dropped me off at Glenn Hills High School. Then, it was up to me to secure a ride home or walk twenty-five miles back home. But I was determined to finish strong with my closest friends.

Summers also provided space to cement our father-son relationship further. Once I completed the assigned homework and did my house chores, I tagged along for a workday in the field with my dad. He was a preferred, seasoned employee of Southern Food Meat Packing Company, a Columbus, Georgia-based business. Drivers frequently tag-teamed Shorty for local routes. As an assisting meat delivery truck driver, he cruised through our county, dropping off frozen goods at our local grocery stores. I highly anticipated the roaring engine of his commercial vehicle on hump-day Wednesday and freedom Friday. Every time these two days rolled around, I jumped out of bed, beyond ready for the upcoming adventures. When Dad hit my neighborhood, he flooded the ambiance with horn honks and gregarious greetings, signaling me to hop on board.

Because Frederick McKinley Jones, an American inventor from Kentucky, leveraged his creativity to invent refrigerated trucks in 1940, his business, Thermo King, still thrives and funds the lifestyle of his heirs. Fast forward a few decades, and this same patented technology allowed men like my father to be gainfully employed. Adults with the foresight to solve problems make substantial headway in progressing family wealth. In hindsight, exposure to his trucking world illustrated the time and wage exchange. Dad earned money for any eight-hour shift and shared his earnings with us. I intuitively learned essential concepts like these in a real-world classroom where my dad was the instructor. The words and actions of parental figures significantly affect a child's development. I am grateful for these fatherly mantras and memories garnered from my rides. His candid insights inevitably laid an essential foundation for my personal advancement. There is perhaps no greater teacher than actual real-world experience.

My high school transition also opened expansive doors in social and financial spaces. I became an ambitious student of America's best science teacher, the one and only Joe L. Scott. Mr. Scott possessed a clever way of explaining the inner workings of atoms and neutrons. The physical body is such an intricate machine. But when we delved into Newton's three laws, he compared them to real-world scenarios, like a rocket launching. A lightbulb lit up. I reprocessed Newton's third law: *for every action, there is an equal and opposite reaction.* For example, if I provide a person with a product, then that consumer gives me the opposite atomic matter: money. What an opportune time to feed my entrepreneurial spirit and expand my business from the chuck wagon to the hallways.

Securing the necessary real estate is the first step in managing a goods-and-services business. Hence, I grabbed my bookbag and headed to the school registrar. After she explained the student list and associated prices, I purchased two adjacent lockers. These two vented rectangles housed my work-life dichotomy, with the first for academics and the second for business. I organized the storefront locker like a modern vending machine, with chocolates at the bottom and chips at the top. This arrangement would keep more perishable items from melting or becoming stale too quickly. I started selling teenage treats the next day to move products and cover my rental fees. I had an entrepreneurial spirit even at such a young, defining age.

Within a few weeks, business was soaring, and I had to scale up to meet the demands. I hired two of my schoolmates, Clarence and Debra. As the chief operating officer, I communicated a clear strategy to my new team. Before the first bell rang, we gathered at the job site, my locker, or the student center. Then, I divided the merchandise among us. Typically, our daily inventory included M&Ms, Nutter Butter, a variety of chips, and Airheads in multiple flavors. At the end of the school day, while most students ran to their buses or the playground, my team and I met up to handle business. After delivering the desired sugar rushes and salty treats to our clients, our profit and loss meetings transpired. We tallied up the goods sold. I collected their earnings and extended my thanks. Then I shared their cut of my profits and gave myself a pat on the back. Any pre-existing friction associated with being a freshman in high school dissipated as my business became a main talking point from hallways to the cafeteria.

Since the students looked to me for additional ways to add thrill to their burgeoning adolescent years, I figured I could leverage my profits to organize school events. Between my sales velocity and social magnitude, staff and students learned who Oz was. Mr. Scott caught wind of my budding business and offered his mentorship. As a realist and a straight shooter, I trusted his advisement. He shared his passionate commitment to economic growth and business development throughout our dialogues. Hence, he had a natural proclivity for young minds like mine that seamlessly subscribed to similar financial pillars. We were the proverbial match made in Heaven.

After class, we united in his room. There, we studied and strategized various avenues to expand my existing business model. Looking at the atomic structures illustrated on the science posters, he emphasized the importance of business. I was the nucleus of my enterprise, charged with keeping my sales force and a diversified product offering in constant orbit. At the close of the meeting, I suggested casino nights at my former elementary school, Ursula Collins. Inside the cafetorium, my trainees and I organized a fun-filled party coined the "Hops." I sourced for a DJ, staffed the concession stand, and applied a five-dollar entry fee. Since the schools were closed on the weekends, I booked our parks and recreational facility, Julian Smith Casino, on any Saturday not reserved for adult bingo. Mr. Scott supervised the events to ensure all attendees enjoyed a safe, grand affair. One night, the weather conditions overshadowed all likelihood of a pleasant experience. A chilling night of about thirty-two degrees hit Augusta. Most parents kept their children home. However, twenty brave souls were willing to bear the frigid conditions and party with us at Julian Smith Casino. After about an hour, the collective body heat failed to mask the cold fog accompanying our conversations. Under the counsel of Mr. Scott, I decided to end the hop early. I refunded all monies. It was better to put the clients first and increase their likelihood of returning for future events.

After calculating my savings, I learned I had enough money for summer school supplies and city-wide commutes. Immeasurable relief and calm refreshed my spirit like a warm summer breeze. Not only did I have sufficient funds to replenish my inventory and cover additional school expenses, but I could also host more events for my clients—dozens of zestful adolescents. Although on a juvenile scale, this business engrained the beauty and pride of being a provider into my psyche. With Dad's accelerating illness and Mom aging gracefully, I found it wise to minimize my asking of Aunt Mattie, with whom I resided. I maximized every summer hour as I embraced increased and self-imposed responsibilities.

For the first two summer school sessions, morning classes kicked off at Glenn Hills High School, at least twenty-five miles from where we lived. The administrator assigned for this two-month educational experience was Mr. Horace Lamback. However, my home school principal, Mr. Barnes, continued to take the lead on my academic success. Ever since my personal introduction to Principal Barnes at my home school, he immediately took a vested interest in my success. Think about Joe Clark, the protagonist in my all-time favorite film, *Lean on Me*, released in 1989. My principal was a living version of him. He ran a tight ship, and every scholar followed his orders. Anyone who entered our doors had to dress for success. From arriving to class on time and exuding scholastic excellence to respecting adults, our principal set a professional, familial tone throughout our school halls. There was no questioning or mistaking; he meant business.

Whether it was during my regularly scheduled school year or summer, Principal Barnes kept his supportive hand on my shoulder. Already privy to my family background and academic hurdles, Mr. Barnes unofficially nominated me as his protege. Under his coaching, I adopted a new perspective on being an astounding man and running an official business. His message was quite simple and concise: Men do the right thing, even when no one is looking. Secondly, buckle down on your studies; stay clear of any trouble. These basic principles further underscored my pre-established familial standards. Moreover, I soundly trusted my silent partner and astute mentor. Within the confines of a public school, activities ranged from learning to fighting. Misplaced rage among young men occasionally exploded as students failed to accept responsibility for their past failures. However, I did not meddle in such conflicts and focused only on my timely graduation. At the close of my second summer session, I scheduled a meeting with Mr. Barnes. When he juxtaposed my needed courses with my attained credits, he happily signed off on my twelfth-grade transition. I did it! Then, he placed an authorization card in my hand, permitting my participation in all senior activities with all privileges. Nothing infused my soul with more gratification than being supported by Augusta's most outstanding educators. At that instant, I could not recall a moment when I experienced more pride.

Growing up under the tutelage of leaders extended beyond the educational setting. I tuned in to my natural inclination for professional environments infused with structure, discipline, and well-dressed adults. I credit my church and childhood mentor, Rev. Clarence Brown, at the Baptist church for this ingrained attraction. I genuinely morphed into a church cornerstone, devoting my Sundays to worship, Mondays to Royal Ambassadors, and Fridays to choir rehearsal. Here, I was assigned multiple leadership roles, for example, the Royal Ambassador. This youth-based program aimed to teach young men about Christ, the principles of God's Word, and the doctrines of church leadership. It was monumental in molding me into the man I am today.

Annual music celebrations added the praise and worship element. Ten to fifteen churches gathered in our sanctuary to celebrate our choir anniversary. As the organ slowed the musical tune, I grabbed the microphone and exclaimed, "Welcome! Beulah Grove Baptist Church, 1434 Poplar Street. Get ready to be astounded by the Young Adult Chorus' exceptional talent!" Sharp hats, ornate dresses, and three-piece suits filled our pews as people readied their souls to praise God. The musical evening was nothing short of amazing, with a competitive resurrection resembling live recordings of the hit TV show *Sunday* Best. When I ran into a citizen in the grocery store or at community events, I would spill a quick infomercial, "Hi, I am Oz. Drop by and witness young people's pure talent and passion as they take the stage and lift their heavenly voices.

You won't want to miss out on this once-in-a-lifetime opportunity!" We always welcomed newcomers with open arms, and I was their delegated spokesman.

Churchgoers of all ages, especially youngsters like me, sought out the beloved Deacon William Howard. Deacon Howard, a wise elder in his seventies, was viewed as the father of our church, the most respected man I witnessed during my childhood. Even when he shared his vocal proclivities via song or hymn, the sanctuary fell silent, moving into the Spirit. This church elder embodied the presumed baritone voice of God. Whenever he uttered a word, you listened; everybody listened. Every listener did precisely what he directed. His voice alone commanded complete attention. Such natural rapport was revered so much that numerous church members considered him their spiritual adviser. His majestic delivery captured the attention of each person with perfect timing. One time, I received an unexpected call from him.

"Hi, Oz. This is Deacon Howard. I know you're having a rough time right now, but I want you to remember this: we're proud of you. You've done some great work here in Augusta; keep your head up. Trust God and focus on your future." Those guiding words dropped in my spirit like the Creator delivered his message vicariously through Deacon Howard that evening. Although I was running on fumes, his timely affirmation fueled my faith, letting me know I could keep going.

According to God's perfect timing, everything happens for a reason, even if we are unaware of the rationale behind an occurrence. Not too long after this spiritual high, I received a debilitating phone call. Unfortunately, my father died when he was only fifty, leaving a vacuum never to be filled. He ascended before I earned my high school diploma, which was a bitter pill to swallow. I recall hearing the news of his death like it was yesterday. I was told he had a heart attack while preparing for his doctor's visit at the VA hospital. It was a tragic turn of events that left us at a dead end. We all moved in shock and grief, feeling like he had been stolen from us so soon. Looking back, it crushes my heart to realize his early extraction from life was preventable. The excessive alcohol use and possibly post-war trauma finally siphoned his life. Yet I treasure the memories of trudging along the delivery routes in the company's enormous truck. I am equally grateful God orchestrated my path to encounter several male role models leading up to my dad's funeral.

After this devastating reality, I continued my high school studies and deeply seated dreams. I gravitated to the Air Force Junior ROTC program. Although I achieved the highest honors throughout high school, I worked to accomplish this prodigious distinction, knowing it inched me closer to my grandest career aspiration. Since the age of thirteen, I have frequently dreamed of serving my country by joining the United States Air Force. I was the First Cadet of the Month at T. W. Josey High School. My high school AFJROTC Instructors, Chief Toole and Major Greer, positively impacted me. These two sharply dressed white men were solid leaders in their Air Force blues. Trust, structure, and standards infiltrated their classroom environment.

Following our midterms, Chief Toole and Major Greer took the cadets on a flight. We boarded a powerful four-engine C130 aircraft designed by Lockheed Martin, an American aerospace and technology corporation. Whether deployed for unprepared runways or transporting military cargo, this was a mighty bird. All fifty of us bravely loaded into the back of the plane and took off. For a moment, the high altitude evoked empowering emotions like I was living on top of the world, moving mountains, and crossing valleys. I was head over heels to explore a career in the sky. Therefore, I joined the Civil Air Patrol, an auxiliary community program, then cast my eyes on the Air Force.

Unfortunately, the chance to make my dreams a reality proved to be an unsuccessful attempt. My Armed Services Vocational Aptitude Battery test scores did not meet the minimum requirement of thirty-six points. Previously, my class promotion to Air Force JROTC Cadet, Squadron Commander, and Cadet Lieutenant Colonel increased my self-esteem tenfold. Yet this isolated failure caused it to dwindle. Heartbroken that my military candidacy was in jeopardy, I began a mental round of second-guessing myself. I tried to take reasonable next steps. Did I do the necessary preparation? Is my dream worth giving that two-hour, thirty-four-minute exam a second shot? Should I retake the ASVAB and focus more on science or arithmetic? I was convinced that paragraph comprehension and word knowledge were grand slams. Thankfully, in another light, wise onlookers deemed me to be a young man suited for the pilot title.

Shortly after attaining my driver's permit, I was officially a junior in high school, on track to graduate in the thirteen years since starting kindergarten. Aunt Mattie and her lifelong best friend, Reann (Re-C) Murry-Grantum, took notice of my wiser-beyond-my-years maturity. My aunt firmly stood her ground by encouraging me to walk, ride a bike, or catch a ride to desired destinations until I reached eighteen blessed years. However, Re-C, akin to a big sister, took a starkly different, albeit risky, approach.

One day, Re-C proposed an irresistibly brilliant idea. Since she worked at Augusta Piedmont Hospital, formerly University Hospital, her schedule was set in stone. Hence, there were twelve-hour time blocks in which her car sat idle in the parking lot. It is not like it had anywhere else it needed to be, so Re-C stepped up for me big time. During certain four-day segments, she graciously allowed me to borrow her car. For a few days a week, I strived to be the best driver in Augusta. Because of her generosity, I never wanted to disappoint her. Whether escorting the elders that I viewed as aunties or spoiling the young lady that carried the title of Oz's sweetheart girlfriend, I kept both hands on the steering wheel at ten and two and obeyed all the rules of the road. In modern times, I would be like a five-star rideshare driver with Moovn Technologies, a bustling Uber competitor.

After being on her feet for twelve hours, handling all blood types and patient personalities, Re-C would enter the passenger side, sit back, and enjoy the ride. This smooth, roaring machine was an immaculate Kelly green 1979 Chevrolet Monte Carlo with the shiniest wheels, a buffed body, and sparkling windows. It always appeared as if it had been freshly driven off the lot.

Since Re-C was also like another aunt in my family, there were lifelong lessons embedded in these extended privileges. As soon as she assumed the posture to lay down the ground rules for using her vehicle, I attuned my ears toward her unwavering voice and paid close attention to every word. Although she was an Oz fan, I knew better than to cross her. Her voice alone commanded respect. Like my esteemed momma and aunt, Re-C meant business. Rule number one was clear as glass: Do not ever arrive late to pick her up from work. I distinctly remember her saying, "Oz, son, when I walk out that door, I better see my car there waiting for me; don't you dare be late, boy!" To be early was to be on time, and I never wanted to lose the afforded driving freedoms. So, I strove to be at least five minutes ahead of schedule every time. It was a privilege to drive her car, and I wasn't about to give her any reason to take back her precious gift to me. Rule number two was equally important: "Make sure I have the exact same amount of gas in my tank as I did when I handed over my keys." Oh, you can bet your money I filled up that tank every day I drove! Failure to do so was a surefire way to get those keys revoked. After all, gas stations were on every corner. I couldn't put a price tag on Re-C's generosity, so I gladly pumped that tank full every chance I got, no excuses.

To ensure I protected her asset, I also employed my own rules. My objectives were to stay under the radar, adhere to the speed limit, and avoid major highways. There was no coloring outside of those lines unless I wanted to risk losing access to the car. Hence, not only was I there to pick her up from work before time by arriving extra early and having a full tank of gas in her car, but I also washed it, making it nice and shiny and super clean. This lessened any anxiety associated with the risk of messing something up. Seeing a pleased look on her face, I could rest a little easier, knowing that I was meeting and exceeding her expectations.

Our special bond blossomed as we made this familial exchange. Perhaps Re-C's trust in me to be a responsible young man in my most embryonic stages of adulthood increased and strengthened my learning curve for the rest of my long road ahead by enabling me to embrace all that it meant to be a man. I learned the importance of time management and respecting other people's property. Whether in my household or in my workplace, I preach and model these same essential soft skills. These are universal abilities that each generation would do well to remember and put into practice. Consistently arriving late for your job or meetings with friends is an unacceptable habit. It shows that you do not value their time when you keep them waiting. Likewise, when you use a meeting room or throw a party at someone else's house, you should always leave the place better than you found it. When someone lends you something, they are already doing you a favor, and common decency dictates that you should, at the very least, return it unharmed.

Even while transitioning to the matriarch of my siblings and me, Re-C dedicated nearly forty years to the hospital. At the time of writing this book, she is still living well, filling the shoes of all my deceased elders. She not only spent nearly forty years working at the hospital but is still a world-class cook. Our relationship is so profound that she shared one of her most coveted and treasured recipes with me. Have you ever attempted to make a pound cake from scratch? Well, she puts any box batter to shame. I am still practicing her perfection to this very day. Perhaps one day, I'll strike it right, and when she bites into my cake attempt, she will smile and say, "Oz, you struck gold." I certainly struck a goldmine by being adopted into her family. She is the epitome of an incredibly strong, compassionate Black woman who single-handedly raised two very productive children. I love her dearly.

Nevertheless, the four-year college commitment was long since forgone, as I had my eyes focused on an immediate mobile goal: a vehicle. This was an objective planted in my spirit by Re-C. Due to her initial compassion toward me at a young, defining age, I garnered an intense taste for being a responsible car owner. You see, becoming a fully grown man in my own right would only be complete if I was trusted to operate as a high-value man. Whether it is a mentor or partner, a person's ability to see that they have arrived at or crossed a certain threshold is measured by the resulting output of multiple inputs in close relationships. A myriad of elders stepped in at the most opportune times and granted me adult-level rights. Their confidence translated into my heightened self-belief to conquer manhood.

Although college was still far from my radar, I devised a solid roadmap. Serving my community and protecting citizens remained a more profound and fervent desire. Hence, I started paying attention to those in my family working with the Sheriff's Department. Watching their positive impact in real time propelled this civic duty to my next choice, only second to the Air Force at the time. In addition, I strategically observed the habits, accolades, and purchases made by outstanding men that steered their lives to rewarding destinations.

Men And Mentors Script The Blueprint

Often, the social conception of when a boy becomes a man collides with an overwhelming need for an alarming revision. Contrary to popular belief in various corners of the world, celebrating an eighteenth birthday, obtaining a high school diploma, or moving into one's home does not define manhood. Instead, a young boy's road to manhood begins day one with an introduction to male adults who can act as role models or mentors. Fortunately, strong male prototypes, including my father, pastors, and educators, were integral to my everyday life. Each man significantly influenced my manhood framework. Aligned with their guidance and constructive criticism, I manufactured a defined mosaic of a successful man.

Leaders, true men of men, are scarce, priceless commodities. Being a man carries its weight of expectations and is an ongoing process. Webster defines man simply as an adult male human with a genetic construct of XY chromosomes. Yet there are so many more distinctive layers, from a racial and socio-economic lens to religious beliefs. Being a Black male in America, my plight was undeniably affected by my background and race. However, I still took complete ownership in shaping my future. A man is a masterful architect who can make a way out of no way. He is resourceful and takes complete ownership of his growth. In short, a man has actionable goals, a heart for the people, and earns a living. His evolution is shaped by ever-changing societal norms, family values, and religious principles. A man must practice mindfulness while being slow to compare, complain, or criticize. He is to hold himself accountable to a greater calling and standard. Most of all, he remains a human with flaws, vices, and strengths. Through the art of self-mastery, a man must extend himself some grace and walk powerfully into a better version of himself. While all these attributes may seem like a tall order, I humbly realize being a fully self-actualized human is an ongoing work in progress. Hence, I constantly seek to better understand and exemplify all it means to be a high-value man, effectively operational in various roles.

Whether a mentor who shared needed success tools, a colleague who pushed me to think creatively, or a friend who stuck by my side through thick and thin, each male figure massively impacted my evolution. I appreciate every person who stimulated my successful rites of passage into manhood. The advice and camaraderie supplied by these working men were essential. Even in the face of adversity, these masculine heroes made time to reaffirm lifelong teachings and offer support. They frequently recognized my excellence and praised my successes, which propelled my budding self-esteem and confidence. Likewise, they routinely pointed out, with grace, where I could grow, encouraging me at every turn to do better and try harder. I attribute a large portion of my success to men who have crossed my path and helped mold me into the man I am today.

Regardless of who they are or where they come from, every impressionable child deserves an uplifting and magnetic Mr. Barnes, Mr. Scott, or Dad. Those relationships were crucial in catapulting me to each career milestone and life success. I am committed to serving as a similar exemplar. After all, every young person needs someone to believe in them, encourage them, and assist them in reaching their greatest potential. Selfless adults who live upright are vital instruments in producing a community of boys and girls equipped to be the best twenty-first-century leaders.

Positive Men Of Influence, Past And Present

I would simply like to pay tribute to those male figures who positively impacted my journey, in one way or another.

Mr. Jeff Annis	Mr. Marion E. Barnes
Mr. Noble Benefield	Mr. Willie Benton
Rev. Dr. Jerry D. Black	Rev. Clarence Brown Sr.
Mr. Mike Brown	Dr. Charles L. Butler
Major Billy Carter	Mr. James Cummings
Rev. Dr. Sam Davis	Mr. Winston Denmark
Mr. Dan G	Mr. William (Gil) Gilyard
Mr. Jay Grover	Mr. Ben Hasan
Mr. Garvin Haynes	Mr. Michael Hightower
Deacon William Howard	Mr. Henry Ingram
Mr. Leroy James	Mr. Anthony Johnson

Mr. Milledge Kyler

Hon. William H. Mays III

Mayor Ed McIntyre

Mr. Ng

Mr. Urbish Patel

Mr. Joe L. Scott

Mr. Clay Sykes

Sgt. E.J. Terry

Chief Charles L. Toole

Dr. Kenneth Walker

Captain Richard Weaver

Commissioner Marion Williams

Mr. Arthur Marshall

Mr. Clinton McGill

Mr. Donald Murphy

Mr. Rocky Patel

Hon. Judge John (Jack) Ruffin

Minnesota (Tim Snell) Fattz

Mr. John Tate

Mr. Bert Thomas

Senator Charles W. Walker

Mr. Tracey Walker

Dr. Hawthorne Welcher

*Alphabetized by last name

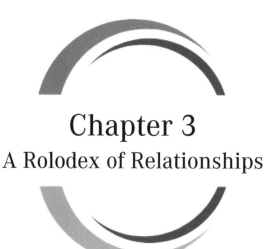

Chapter 3
A Rolodex of Relationships

A s the earth tilted towards the sun and spring transitioned to summer, the global economy of 1985 drastically shifted. Residing in the United States in the late seventies compared to the early eighties was like night and day. Despite aggressive governmental efforts, such as Reaganomics and tax cuts, put in force to lighten the financial blows of a recession-plighted seventies, the United States still experienced the infiltration of monetary deficits. Countless fiscal variables were simultaneously at play. After a grueling, twenty-year Vietnam war, a seventy percent increase in oil prices, and a laundry list of other restraints, everyday citizens and mid-size businesses were too far behind the eight ball to catch up. It would take a Hail Mary to revitalize their positive trajectory. One could only hope.

According to the American Bankruptcy Institute, from 1980 to 1985, following the Bankruptcy Reform Act, nearly two million businesses, including farmers, filed for bankruptcy. Typically, these legal proceedings are only executed as a last hope method to surviving suffocating financial whirlwinds. Outstanding debts and financial obligations exceeded gross profits and net pay. This economic downturn was only the beginning. Unfortunately, the government's bold attempt to curve indebtedness and keep businesses open only slowed the onset of another recession. Companies like Rich's department store, which formerly agreed to cover unbacked checks written by Atlanta teachers after the Great Depression and allowed sit-ins for leaders protesting segregation and economic inequities during the 1960s, was acquired by Federated department stores just a few years prior. Dire financial stressors forced businesses and citizens to sell off assets and make legacy-shifting decisions to merely survive. Another testing decade of unemployment in tandem with rampant inflation set family dynamics, monetary cushions, and short-term goals afire.

Unfortunately, gainfully employed adults suddenly found themselves overqualified, unemployed, or underemployed, all within one quarter. The hopeful dependence on bimonthly pay cycles cascaded into a disabling pool of layoffs. By God's saving grace, I avoided the first round of cross-country financial demise and jobless status that knocked down families' stability like a dreadful nuclear explosion leaving nothing in its wake. Initially, my entry-level job pursuits insulated me from such economic turmoil. Fresh out of high school, my financial obligations were minimal, but I craved the working-man title. Generating wages of my own volition in exchange for an hourly commitment spoke volumes to me. The sheer chance of walking into the bank to cash a check that read, "Pay to the order of Oz Nesbitt," excited me beyond belief. Of course, like many green young adults, I had my head nestled in the clouds of possibilities. My lofty dreams far outweighed my current reality.

As soon as I caught wind of a downtown job opening on Augusta's busiest block, I wasted not a moment and applied. Before I could fully indulge in a summer break of pure relaxation, Ruben's department store on Broad Street offered me a full-time position, and of course, I gladly accepted. Established in 1889, Ruben's was a popular community mainstay that offered timeless fashion to people of all shapes, sizes, and ages across all income streams. This red brick establishment showcased its latest, distinguished styles via the plastic mannequins propped in the full-sized picture windows. These full-body synthetic replicas of stylish citizens highlighted the most desired seasonal wardrobes with budget-friendly price tags.

Much like Rich's, Ruben's carried assorted accessories and clothing for men, women, boys, and girls. With such inclusivity, Ruben's survived in unstable market conditions. In fact, it still stands strong even today. On any given day, it was highly probable that a full-time employee would cater to a diverse clientele ranging from eight to ninety-eight years old, each with starkly different preferences and budgets. Grandmothers sent any suit-wearing, Bible-toting man to this apparel landmark, which reeked of Old Spice and Copenhagen colognes. Here, men metamorphosed into the well-dressed, high-value collective by the standards of any fashion-savvy onlooker. Contrarily, on the opposite end of the age spectrum, grandchildren hand-selected gifts for well-dressed family members too. From its inception, this department store became a cross-generational staple in the Augusta community, much like Rich's was in Georgia's prominent capital of Atlanta.

During the work week, I emerged from bed before sunrise to prepare myself for the working man's lifestyle. Remember, to be early is to be on time. To be on time is to be late. Hence, I strove to be the first one to clock in. Suited with my best blazer, I did a double take at my reflection, spritzing on my Halston cologne. Then, I paused in admiration of my gig line execution. The way the seam of my button-up shirt aligned with my belt buckle and trouser zipper was almost straighter than the line Jesus walked. Sure, that may be a slight exaggeration, but I keenly observed a vertical, 180-degree line in the mirror. Not only was I dressed for success, but I confidently presumed my former teachers and current mentors would give a firm nod of approval. My new morning routine was off to an outstanding start, with a positive attitude, approach, and appearance in motion.

As soon as I crossed the kitchen threshold, the scent of soul food flooded my senses. My grandmother and I exchanged hugs, followed by a warm "good morning." I can still hear her compassionate voice after all these years. Then, I eagerly sat down to pray before gratefully consuming a warm bowl of grits with a piece of her mouth-watering fried chicken. Home-cooked meals made with unwavering love usually held me over until I returned home for supper. Grandma and Aunt Mattie wished me well before sending me off to my first employment experience. To reach my destined workplace, I either caught a ride or hiked five miles on my own two feet. No distance was too long for me to earn a dollar and honor my contractual agreement. Additionally, I was in remarkable shape and filled with an innate drive to secure my rightful spot in manhood.

Once I clocked in, the gentlemen's hour commenced. I craftily pieced looks together for a mature demographic, including men between forty to seventy years of age. From Sebago shoes and Levi jeans to tailored blazers and collared shirts, helping men from all walks of life achieve their best look was gratifying, to say the least. Most fellas sought an outfit for Sunday church services, graduations, or weddings. After measuring their size and understanding their vision, I offered clients a few pairing options. For example, a few clients preferred slim-fitting pinstriped suits with a nice bow tie suitable for a more formal affair. On the contrary, a sweater vest and khaki pants met the fashion mark for the typical weekend outing. Within a few short weeks, my versatility in wardrobe assemblies and customer service heightened, and so did my efficiency. To think of it, I could probably get a man in and out of the store, dressed perfectly for an important occasion, within forty-five minutes or less. By observing his stature, the car he drove, and the aura he exuded, I could discern the best fit that would match that brother's personality. It paid handsomely to be insightful and attentive.

Ruben's not only provided my first paycheck, but it also uncovered a deeply rooted phobia: cats. Outside of Peggy Nesbitt or God Himself, no other atomic creation, eternal or not, could cause my heart to race faster than a Brazilian jaguar. Like twenty percent of individuals in the United States, the sight of cats caused heightened blood pressure and clouded vision. Whenever I entered my workspace, my ailurophobia came into play the instant I spotted any of the five Persian felines freely roaming around as if they owned the place. This was their rightful territory. They lurked around as if they owned every square foot of that blessed store! As a person who preferred predictability and stability, the feline mammal group existed on different terms. Cats can shift from calm, purring creations to feisty, leaping attackers in the blink of an eye. Luckily for me, Ruben's cats were accustomed to people. Usually, they curled up in a corner on the top floors. Yet, on the few sporadic days when these furry little devils disguised as fluffy, cute creatures prowled along the first floor, I combatted uncomfortable anxiety instead of assisting clients. Subconsciously, I understood that at any unpredicted moment, a simple staring contest between a cat and me could transform into an unfair brawl. While I never pinpointed an exact phobia-causing stimulus that initiated this innate, prominent fear, successfully acquiring an animal-free work environment inched closer to a top priority.

Before the close of a prosperous summer, the opportunity to escape phobia-prone scenarios and increase my hourly wages arose. My friend Chuck, who also worked downtown, shared a new job opportunity with me. Two weeks prior, he had resigned from a business adjacent to Ruben's. Then, he started working at a new company on the opposite side of town, near Augusta Regional Airport at Bush Field. When he rapidly recounted his daily duties of working in a manufacturing plant, such as making printed and designed fabrics, the job transition spoke softly. I was not impressed. So, I resumed rehanging and folding the tried-on garments scattered throughout the men's department. Yet when he mentioned a $12-per-hour starting pay, I tuned in and was sold. A plausible wage increase was sweet music to my ears. It captivated my soul, much like "Papa's Got a Brand-New Bag," a Grammy Award-winning song by Augusta's own James Brown, which also reached the Billboard Top

100 list. Who would not want a larger bag of money coupled with more disposable income? I certainly did!

As a recent graduate, making more money in the same eight-hour period would fuel my savings and expedite the attainment of my personal goals. After my shift ended at Ruben's, Chuck and I headed toward the airport to drop off my application. While I continued working at Ruben's to save money, I banked on seizing this new opportunity coupled with increased cash flow. Within two weeks, I, too, landed a blue-collar job with Textron Textiles Industries, also known as T.T.I., located on Dixon-Airline Road in South Augusta. I was beyond grateful the stars seemed to align. God's grace fell upon my interview process.

Watching the threads and yarn spin together to create one sheet symbolized the way life was stringing together for me. Before long, my presence was viewed as a considerable asset to T.T.I.'s supply chain efforts. I was found driving forklifts and heavily involved in production. Whenever a coworker called out, I ensured business flowed as needed and volunteered to fill their shoes, plus mine. I tackled any duty thrown in my direction without a flinch. More tenured employees declined additional workloads that did not include overtime pay. They were comfortable executing the same work tasks five days a week, and rightfully so. However, I welcomed the opportunity to heighten my learning curve. Those vested workers would not see my teenage ego back down from a new challenge. I was always up for whatever task they gave me. Maybe I appeared irrational to them, but little did they know I was tenaciously building my resume, hollowing out my rightful place in the world.

As soon as I reached the ninety-day mark at T.T.I., I verified my checking account balance, then caught a ride to Gerald Jones Honda on Gordon Highway. The perfect moment to pick out my first vehicle was here. Of course, the sales agent showed me a few cars above my five-thousand-dollar price point, but I only wanted a car with a historical track record of lasting forever. That wasn't unreasonable, right? Then, there it was. It was a shining burnt orange 1983 Honda Accord hatchback. The interior offered a plush gray fabric in mint condition, plus a Panasonic cassette player. Talk about top-of-the-line! After bargaining with the salesman, I exited the dealership with keys in hand. Another mark of becoming an independent and successful man was accomplished. Check!

From that point on, I enjoyed a fresh-air commute to South Augusta, Monday to Friday. I eagerly rolled down the front windows with every ounce of my forearm muscle. My physical workout continued once I arrived at T.T.I. Since our manufacturing plant operated as one of the top three suppliers to national brands like Joann's Fabrics, meeting production quotas and deadlines were two non-negotiables. From bed linen to fine upholstery, our warehouse location maintained a stronghold on wholesale partnerships with large retail stores. When the conveyor belt rolled out a perfectly color-contrasting G.I. Joe and Daffy Duck dye print from our children's inventory, I smiled and abruptly paused. As I recalled the leading roles of these cartoon characters, it highlighted my dreams as a young lad. There will be no more playing small in hopes of securing overtime. It was time to pull up my bootstraps, and consciously transform into a supernatural protagonist in my life story.

Sure, the biweekly checks paid my bills, but they would do little to position me as the breadwinner for my future family. My aspirations were distinctly higher. I was obviously not operating in my genius zone. These work roles did not feed my purpose. Unfortunately, I was expending energy working odd-end jobs, but I believed a positive plot twist was on the horizon. I held out hope.

After the holiday peak season ended, I noticed the workforce getting slimmer and slimmer by the week. Yet, I remained committed to my job, showing up fifteen minutes early and meeting each production quota set forth weekly. One day, I was baffled when I eyed my shift manager on our floor. Then, he called my name. When I received a pink slip, my heart dropped to the pit of my stomach. I suddenly realized I was just a number on a budget line rather than indispensable, just another cog in a big wheel of moving gears. This realization may have been a shock to my system, but it opened my eyes to the capitalistic ways engrained in this dog-eat-dog world. My worldview and need for financial agility were expanded. Faithfully, I trusted my supreme Provider that my employment status would be but a temporary hiccup. Nonetheless, a little anxiety crept into my spirit. I am human, after all. I had just purchased my brand-new vehicle. Plus, the rent was due. Living expenses did not cease just because my paycheck did. Hence, securing a stable source of income was critical.

On this calamitous evening, I decelerated, slowly cruising into Glendale Subdivision. Then, I parked on the corner and walked over to the forty-foot magnolia tree rooted in the center of Aunt Mattie's flourishing yard. Given the forecasted rains, it would be time to rake the leaves and cut the grass again this Saturday. *Maybe I could start a lawn care business to hold me over until I found a new job, or I could collect dozens of plums in the backyard and sell them at a local farmers market,* I pondered. Solution-based ideas ran rapidly in my mind, as carrying the title of unemployed was an unacceptable reality for me. My crafty brain was churning out ideas again, much like in high school when I ran my lucrative business of selling candy bars and chips out of a locker. Being cash-poor or solely dependent on unemployment checks was far from my peripheral vision.

Once I mustered up the energy to enter the house, my nostrils were hit with the soulful scent of fried pork chops, black-eyed peas, and collard greens: a cultural staple known to incite thoughts of monumental abundance. I passed the floor furnace. Aunt Mattie's fragrance of rose and neroli notes met my olfactory glands. It was time to face the music. I took a deep breath and faithfully walked into her master bedroom, ready to confront this adverse reality.

"Hi, Aunt Mattie. I have to find a job," I confessed, my gaze fixated on her facial expression as my thumbs twiddled.

"Well, hello, Oz." She moved calmly to the corner edge of her bed. "What on earth happened, nephew?"

I mustered my strength to maintain her steadfast gaze and explained, "T.T.I. completed another round of layoffs. Unfortunately, the popular human capital management practice, last hired and first fired, picked my employee number today. I guess my time was up."

I can still remember hearing that sound in her voice: you know that sound of frustration and disgust your parents have from time to time. It's like this pivotal conversation happened just yesterday.

The inevitable sound when elders fight back the urge to say, "I told you so," although the statement would be quite befitting. Her long pause underscored the possibility that she remained a strong proponent of my higher education pursuits. From her three-degrees-achieved lens, I should have enrolled in college right after my high school graduation. By entertaining a leap year and forgoing a degree, I had wasted the past several months in an unstable working world. Yet, she kept these supposed thoughts to herself and continued actively engaging in our conversation.

Then, with a caring and intentional stare, she asked, "Well, what do you wanna do?"

Slightly nervous about conveying a professional transition to a livelihood of imminent danger, I inched closer to her. Then, I leaned in to share my newly discovered ambitions.

I responded, "I think I want to become a police officer."

Without the slightest degree of hesitation, she reached for her rotary telephone on the bedside table and replied, "Let me call Charles."

I had no recollection of who Charles was or how this call would play an integral part in my newfound career aspirations.

What I did know was Ms. Mattie Burney, who I affectionately called Aunt Mattie, knew thousands of people. Not only that, but she also made it her duty to know the right people. Aunt Mattie was an iconic queen of massive action and purposeful connections. Within our close-knit community, she wore many hats and did so quite powerfully. Additionally, my mom's only sister attained her master's degree and educational specialist degree during a time of extreme oppression. Fast forward, this thirty-three-year veteran educator was also an acclaimed city gem. Her no-nonsense presence commanded attention in any room. She moved with pure intentions.

She buzzed Senator Charles Walker and explained what was going on. I had passionately expressed my desire to become a police officer. Then, she handed me the phone.

Senator Walker's astute voice said into my ear, "If you're serious about getting into law enforcement, young man, we need to kick off your career at the Sheriff's Department, not the City Police." Back in the day, two primary law enforcement agencies existed: the Augusta Police Department and the Richmond County Sheriff's Department. Senator Walker told me when to be at his office.

At that time, State Senator Charles Walker was a highly sought-after leader throughout Georgia. This Augusta College graduate and US Navy veteran, Charles Walker, exemplified the beautiful intersection of entrepreneurship and education against the backdrop of community empowerment. Walker conveyed his unwavering determination to dismantle systemic oppression via his newspaper, *The Augusta Focus*. Then, in 2015, he authored *From Peanuts to Power* to illustrate how descendants of sharecroppers can move to owning company shares across multiple industries. Needless to say, Senator Walker was a busy man making nation-shifting moves. He was an unbought, unbossed leader who operated with a pull-yourself-up-from-your-bootstraps work ethic akin to civil rights leader Hosea Williams. That said, even while juggling fatherhood, enterprises, and politics, he still cleared his calendar for little Oz. I considered myself both humbled and honored.

After hanging up the phone that momentous day, I profusely thanked my dear Aunt Mattie, hugging her close, inhaling her familiar, comforting scent, and feeling grateful once again to have her as my second mother.

The following morning, I dressed in my best suit and left an hour earlier than our scheduled meeting. I was no novice to professional decorum. First impressions could bring life or death to budding relationships. My initial visit to State Representative Walker's office on the corner of Wrightsboro Road and 12th Street remains unforgettable to this very day. Adjacent to W&H Income Tax Service and the Black Focus Newspaper, a glass window read his name and title. Once I entered the office and introduced myself, the office manager escorted me to the senator's office. As he looked me over to assess my attire, mindset, and hunger, he posed a few questions. Then, he pivoted around in his big executive-style chair and pressed one button on his telephone behind his cherry-oak desk.

In an affirmative tone, he stated, "Sheriff, I got a young man who I think will make us a fine deputy." He nodded and hung up.

I sat there, on the edge of my seat, wondering what the sheriff had uttered.

"You're in luck; you just need to submit your official application," the senator said with a smile.

I gulped to swallow my immeasurable anticipation. I could hardly believe my good fortune.

"Thank you, sir," I replied with a firm handshake, telling him he wouldn't regret giving me this lifeline.

"Do your community proud, son, and you will have made me proud," he affirmed as I exited his office.

Just like that, with the snap of a finger and well-connected trailblazers, my life's trajectory changed three days later. I was hired in full uniform, gun and all. Although the standard uniform fell loosely upon my one-hundred-fifty-pound slim frame, I embodied a robust posture like a certified community hero. Whatever fate presented, I would handle it all with wisdom and integrity. This position quickly thrust me into becoming the youngest Black, most popular, high-profile law enforcement officer between 1985 and 2000.

Relationships Are Prized Gatekeepers

Decades ago, five degrees of separation existed between a person one befriended and the decision-maker one needed to know. Relationships continue to reign as invaluable assets in life. Senator Charles W. Walker became my prized mentor. He schooled me on the good, bad, and not-so-good in life and politics—the downright ugly and blasphemous, you might say. This introduction was made possible by my biological connection to Aunt Mattie. Now, the reality has significantly changed, especially given one billion social media users and only one person stands between you and a golden opportunity. The missing link between a historical relationship could very well be the person looking back at you in the mirror. Never underestimate your connections and the influencers linked to them.

As Grandma would wisely express, "Don't mess around and get amnesia." Such a thoughtless act is one cardinal sin I would never commit. My actions alone would reply, "Well, Grandma, I never did and never will forget my humble beginnings." On numerous occasions, I mirrored that same networking fervor of Aunt Mattie. Without hesitation, I filled the gap for those in need and blessed others. I was eager to throw a lifeline to anyone, especially in my younger, naïve years. The hero complex was ingrained and prominent. Moreover, paying it forward is a natural duty of a good Samaritan. Isn't that what Jesus did? In a similar vein, I continue to live my life.

Through experiences, I painfully learned and am equally humbled to know I am not the omnipotent One equipped to save everyone. With that withstanding, I vigorously work to add value to the majority. From the school-aged child to Social Security recipients, with more wisdom and discernment, I continue to bless people along my journey, meeting them where they are. After all, God has blessed me abundantly, so it is only right I pay it forward. God gives everyone gifts to use for the betterment of humanity and to bring Him glory.

"Favor ain't fair" is commonly toted by those like me, who do not take their success for granted. Whether a person is born with a silver spoon or a humbling wooden one in their mouth, odds will be stacked against them, sometimes making massive success appear as an impenetrable wall. However, even if this barrier is concrete strengthened with metal rebar, it is breakable to a believer walking by faith. People and places along an ambitious pathway come together to create the perfect bridge to one's next best opportunity. It's not about who is most worthy, smart, or wealthy, but about embracing God's promises bestowed upon your life.

Being in close proximity to ingenious elders and progressive entrepreneurs keeps me sharp. If I review my laundry list of accomplishments, I can credit a large percentage of those victories to my inner circle and network. Such influential individuals allowed God to position them for my benefit and scaffold me to the next level of greatness. By the same token, I am beyond grateful God deemed me worthy and ordered my every step. Whatever career field one chooses, the right relationships are the fourth essential need for survival after food, water, and shelter. As Senator Walker proclaimed, "There are no permanent friends and no permanent enemies." Never allow short-term experiences or disagreements to burn a bridge. That bridge may very well be a life-saving path over troubled waters leading to a transformative victory. Leverage your discernment; extend forgiveness where warranted.

Remember, securing the first interview, climbing the ladder to upper management, and building a seven-figure legacy are highly predicated on who you know more than what you know. We carry the collective responsibility of extending our network to others. It is via intentional collaborations we can elevate nations and fortify legacies. But it all starts with one small action: the firm decision to take the first step. Do it and keep forging forward.

Chapter 4
On Duty for a Greater Purpose

While Atlanta-based Coca-Cola was taking its first shot at modifying its century-old formula with the addition of corn syrup, adventurous individuals were launching businesses and exercising their talents throughout the eighties. Regardless of age, people sought a matching caffeine charge that naturally resulted from taking big risks. For example, in 1985, shortly after demonstrating his incredible athleticism during his first year with the Chicago Bulls, Michael Jordan was crowned the NBA's Rookie of the Year. Because Jordan took this leap of faith and paused his collegiate education at The University of North Carolina, just one year shy of graduation, he achieved this historic accomplishment. Between scoring three-pointers and studying for his remaining courses, Jordan graduated in 1986. Then, he skillfully became the first player since Wilt Chamberlain to score over 3000 points in a single season. Meanwhile, on my personal court, after nearly two years of hopping around between odd-end jobs while keeping my head above the economic downturns, it was my optimal turn to take my shot. I planted myself into a steady career and endured a downpour of first-time experiences.

At the crack of dawn, I pulled my ash-gray pants and blue collared shirt from my bedroom closet. Then, I grabbed the can of starch and plugged in the iron. As I creased the lines to hit perfectly at my knee, I smiled at my ability to sport this civic duty uniform for the next eight-hour shift. There was no doubt in my mind that Chief Toole, my J.R.O.T.C. instructor from high school, would again approve of my gig line. Suiting up to ace a class and protect my community was the same routine—only the uniform changed.

Being a young, energetic, and well-spoken deputy who took great pride in wearing my uniform and badge, I coveted my new role and the training ground it afforded me during my first two years. As a jailor, I routinely looked to my superiors for guidance. Lieutenant Tom Mason, a mature white man, who had established a legendary career as a patrolman, was assigned to the same precinct. Due to a work-related injury, he was reassigned as a police firearms instructor. From the moment we met, he morphed into a sort of father figure and expressed a strong desire for me to achieve the highest honors possible. He patiently and diligently taught me how to handle a firearm, leading me to the notable achievement of marksmanship. Following months of world-class training with Lieutenant Mason, I exceeded a 60% hit count in slow fire and a 50% hit count in timed fire against a seven-yard target. Although my aim increased with more shooting practice, my goal was to de-escalate every situation, ensuring that it never escalated to the point where I needed to draw my firearm. This nonviolent approach should be the case for all officers proudly serving their communities. All firearms should only be employed as a last resort.

Before reaching my second anniversary with the police force, I was introduced to Captain Richard Collins Weaver in 1986, a graduate of T.W. Josey High just like me. When I listened to him narrate the role of those in public service with such magnetism at a road patrol briefing, I thought to myself, *Wow, he is a stellar leader.* He was a tall, middle-aged Black deputy who had climbed the ranks. Whenever I saw Captain Weaver, he exhibited a positive attitude. He sported a well-groomed appearance, always sharply dressed in his uniform, finished with freshly shined shoes. At that time, he was the highest-ranking Black deputy, later promoted to the rank of Major. Not only was he a proud, God-fearing, churchgoing, devoted husband, and father with a noticeable vested interest in the betterment of our community, but he was also an accessible, down-to-earth leader who willfully offered guidance to rookies like me. He quickly evolved into my esteemed mentor, encouraging me to enroll in offered training, such as Report Writing, Hostage Negotiations, and Crime Scene Investigations. I was indebted to working under the tutelage of this Vietnam War veteran.

Major Weaver mentored me on navigating the wars within the workplace and those that spur over into our county. With a direct connection to his historical progress, I deemed it quite plausible I, too, could be Sheriff one fateful day. These aspirations were shared with a few special family members and friends. Those within my bloodline supported my aspirations and cautioned me to always be vigilant at work. Conversely, a few friends and foes got wind of my lofty dreams. They were not happy campers. Some more tenured officers began treating me like a castaway. The handwriting was clearly written on the wall in large and clear letters. It was simply unwise to share my career dreams any further. Tension and microaggressions spread, but I remained humble and committed to my job. It is important to remember no matter what you do in life, do it with humility. Do not give any haters room to live rent-free in your head.

At every interval in which worry and stress peaked, God found a way to infuse my week with immense laughter. Perhaps, that can be attributed to the biblical verses that illustrate how the Lord works in mysterious ways. While patrolling Gordon Highway, a car flew past me like it aimed to beat William "Bubba" Wallace, the second Black driver to win at NASCAR's elite Cup level since Wendell Scott in 1963. Every speed limit sign clearly stated forty-five miles per hour, yet this driver had her metal foot fully engaged on the gas pedal. When I clocked her speed, the speed radar gun read seventy miles per hour. I did a double take, blinked in pure disbelief, then flipped on my siren. Once she noticed I was tailing her, she slowly pulled off the closest exit into the parking lot.

I approached her driver's side window. "Ma'am, what's the hurry?"

She sunk in her seat in disappointment and grabbed her stomach, "Well, Deputy, you may not believe me, but I've got a severe case of diarrhea. If I do not make it a restroom now, I am going to have an awfully big mess to clean up."

I fought back the urge to say, "TMI, lady," and instead said, "I understand, ma'am; let me just see your license and registration. Then, you can run inside this gas station."

She pulled a badge that confirmed she was an official army major.

I quickly tapped her car. "Thank you for your service, ma'am; you can go."

Since Fort Gordon Military Base was in Augusta, I speculated she might have been heading in that direction. The balance of atrocities and humor fueled my adulting engine and counteracted plausible breaking points that stemmed from such a highly demanding, low-paying job.

Not only did my role in law enforcement give me free rein throughout Richmond County, but it also showed onlookers you could shift society's view of the Black man in America. All too often, media outlets and old Jim Crow laws prevailed in the Deep South. Black men were viewed as criminals and drug addicts instead of leaders and officers. Yes, even well into the twentieth century, still today, racism can run rampant. In fact, staggering incarceration rates only underscore the predicament marginalized groups fall into like a choking sinkhole. The Sentencing Project, based in Washington, D.C., found Black Americans are incarcerated at five times the rate of white Americans. Such alarming numbers further economic disparities and familial instabilities. Hence, five days a week, I took complete authority in reshaping this flawed narrative and exemplifying the powerful qualities of being a Black man entrusted to uphold the law. Unfortunately, my equitable perspective was not shared by all.

Early in my career, working alongside certain officers blurred my usually optimistic lens. During a routine patrol, a call came in that a teenager was not in school. A fellow white deputy decided to teach this child a painful lesson. Once he located the student, he forcibly threw him to the ground. Lying there face down, in tears, his slim body became a soccer ball. The deputy at hand reared his leg back and kicked him in the rib cage, not once, but twice, while yelling the word "nigger." Talk about adding insult to injury. Meanwhile, in a state of utter vulnerability, this innocent young man cradled his head in his arms and pleaded, "Please stop, please." It was like a dreadful horror movie playing out before my eyes in slow motion, but the cruel reality was that it was a real terroristic act.

Once I arrived on the scene, I jumped out of my car and sprinted to them. Before he could violently land another blow, I firmly grabbed my colleague's arm. "Hey, man, that's enough. That's a child you're battering."

He dismissively replied, "Shucks, he made me get dirty mud splatters on my uniform I just picked up from the cleaners." Like a heartless human, he failed to realize that brutally stomping in drenched dirt and wrestling someone's unarmed son to the wet grass were the real culprits of his dirty attire, not to mention a result of his equally dirty attitude.

From my point of view, these blotches represented the internal toxicity and immaturity circulating in his soul. This deputy had no license to cause harm to anyone, let alone a civilian who posed no imminent danger. Such a stark incident was proof some stains do not come off easily. These dangerous prejudices are so ingrained in one's soul. It takes one trigger to expose a man for who he truly is. We can often judge a person's innermost character by how they treat those who they perceive as inferior, whether based on a disadvantage, class, age, or whatever. Take your pick.

Of course, such heinous acts did not sit right with me. I decried the overuse of deadly force. What would have happened if this same deputy had called for backup and the officer who showed up shared his race-driven biases? In hindsight, he should have handcuffed himself for disorderly conduct and assault. Nevertheless, I was determined to hold him accountable after rescuing one child from his rage. Once we returned to the police precinct, I immediately filed an official complaint at my boss's office. This other deputy's unapologetic and blatant act of racism was deeply disturbing. Unfortunately, his inhumane acts were only met with a written reprimand and a three-day suspension without pay. It was my hope that missing out on his light bill money would force him to address his hidden biases. Within the confines of that devastating work shift, my role transformed into an unstated dual function: protecting citizens from each other and guarding citizens against badge-carrying racists. Standing up to confront racism head-on allowed me to channel my empathy and desire for true independence.

Building family bonds while maintaining a home was second nature to my mother and Aunt Mattie. Hence, it was a bittersweet moment when I decided to leave the nest, but it was time. As Matthew, Chapter 19 says, "And a man shall leave his father and mother and join his wife: and they too shall become one." My first marriage marked the genesis for me to form my personal family unit. Although my village did a remarkable job raising me, I took immense pride in building my own family. After a small, quaint wedding, my first wife, along with my first child, Oz Jr., brought this goal to fruition.

A few blocks from Prestige Automotive Dealership, Southgate Apartments won me over after a quick tour. It housed a younger demographic, but nonetheless, the renters were working-class and family oriented. Once I received the golden keys to my first place, I gazed at the bare walls of this two-bedroom apartment. Then, I immediately took a drive to my mom's place. Along this twenty-mile ride, I reflected on the increased responsibilities I assumed.

My firsthand experience as the head of the household shined a light on my novice financial acumen. The rent was $750 a month. Reality hit me with force akin to a steel wrecking ball aimed at demolishing the tallest skyscraper in Dubai. However, in my everyday world, I miscalculated the full price of leading the ideal household I mentally engineered prior to moving. This expedited my learning curve and my need to lean on family.

Mom shared a list of necessary cleaning supplies, such as bleach, Comet, and Windex, in tandem with recommended grocery stores. As I scouted out different deals and groceries, my wife cooked the daily meals. Yet when the weekend arrived, I resumed the role of head chef. Numerous financial gurus proclaim eating at home cuts expenses by 20%. But there was a larger problem at hand: we did not have enough cash flow. A person can only cut so much and still have a decent standard of living. There was more month than money.

Living on my own for the first time made that abundantly clear. Hence, I had to rely on my ability to lean on our omnipotent Provider.

Since I opted not to get any secondhand items from local consignment shops or family, it was up to me to find creative ways to furnish our new place. Mom ran down a laundry list of three or four reputable stores, all located in the same ten-mile radius along Broad Street. I cranked up my vehicle, recounted the two hundred dollars in my wallet, then headed downtown. Once I turned left onto the eleven hundredth block, I entered the first store, Benson's Furniture Company. Since no one was there to greet me or offer any assistance, I took a stroll around the showroom. I mentally decorated my living room in my photographic memory, working to identify which items complemented one another. I continued to gather ideas, notating price tags.

Then, suddenly, a raspy voice asked, "Son, how can I help you?"

When I turned around, there was an older white guy dressed in a pinstriped collared shirt seated near the large glass window facing the street.

We walked toward each other.

I assuredly replied, "Yes, sir, my mom sent me down here to select some furnishings for my new apartment."

He curiously asked, "What's your momma's name?"

"Ms. Peggy Nesbitt, sir," I proudly answered, grinning ear to ear. Just saying my good birth-giver's name brought a smile to my face.

Before responding, he mustered up just enough energy to stand up halfway. His illustration of excitement conveyed their trusted, long-term acquaintance.

Then, he yelled to an associate, motioning for him to join us urgently. "Listen, you get this boy whatever he wants in this building!"

After testing the comfortability of sofa sets and their associated pricing, I selected the best living room suite. It was a burgundy leather sofa with plush cushions and an accompanying loveseat. I also tacked on two halogen floor lamps.

The grand total was double the amount I anticipated, but the store manager introduced me to their finance program. Like most young adults, my credit score was subpar, yet on the strength of my mother's name alone, I could afford the world. After carefully reading over the terms, I signed a carbon copy contract. Abundantly flowing with gratitude, without making a single downpayment, I furnished my family room for the meager cost of $25 a month. What a budget-friendly deal; it was practically a steal! My mother's reputation equated to strong name recognition with any downtown merchant. Her clout subjectively cosigned my lending agreement.

Not only did I view this credit opportunity as a chance to build my financial worthiness, but a large part of my motivation was also to avoid piercing pain and ego stabs. Although I no longer lived under my mother's roof, a slight fear of her wrath remained rooted deep into my chest cavity. It would be embarrassing and ego-piercing if the owners called my momma due to missed payments. At that moment, the prolific power of integrity and character was magnified.

I learned firsthand that your word is your bond. Body language, including a firm handshake and eye-to-eye verbalization, proved sufficient. These same communicative tools translated to the professional realm as well.

During my law enforcement tenure, my reputation as a speaker became well-known in the community as I evolved into a neighborhood staple for using my voice to reach people across the aisles. At five a.m., I had the pleasure of serving as the morning traffic reporter on the local C.B.S. affiliate and the local Urban Radio Station. This media opportunity ignited at Beulah Grove Baptist Church. When I shared the pulpit with my progressive pastor on Easter, I realized my dreams were not dead. Once I proclaimed with great reverence, "He has risen," all church members rose from their pews and sang praises to God. Easter speeches evolved into school announcements, then morning traffic news. To persistently nurture this gift, I joined Toastmasters in my early twenties and accepted various speaking engagements. My profound affinity for career advancements and community duties was progressively expanding.

Also, during this transitional season, my lifelong crush, Robernett, had re-entered my ever-evolving world. Since the tender age of eight, I have admired and flirted with this royal lady. She was the most poised, elegant, beautiful girl I had ever laid eyes on during my elementary school days. Although we were simply children at Ursula Collins Elementary School, my stomach fluttered like a black butterfly when she first crossed my path. Named after a prominent African American female principal, our school has educated thousands of low-income minority students since the 1970s. Those four walls housed thousands of ambitious children excited to master essential reading, writing, and calculating skills. Meanwhile, identifying avenues to see Robernett was another venture that excited me more than a kid at a candy store.

One day, after wrapping up Easter practice, I witnessed a cutie with ponytails and hair bows exiting a neighboring church, Mount Zion Baptist. Although she wore age-appropriate clothing and hairstyles, she resonated with womanhood from a distance. Immediately, I felt an uncontainable attraction as I stopped in my footsteps. Robernett was a slim, tall girl who exuded high standards and style even as a fifth grader. She matched my gaze, then continued to enter her mother's green car. Fingers crossed, and faith peaked, I gazed into the heavens from the lawn of my home church, Beulah Grove Baptist. I hoped and prayed to see this beautiful flower again.

Even as a young, wide-eyed seventh grader, I decided to take the lead to see where this entrancing stare would carry us. One of my best friends, Monique, also had an established friendship with Robernett. Monique was like the little sister I never had and the daughter of Aunt Mattie's best friend. Hence, although two years apart in age, we were like two brown peas in a pod. Once I confessed my after-church experience to her, Monique fed me insider information, hoping this beautiful girl would tie the knot with her brother-friend. As luck would have it, I memorized Robernett's route and preferences. For the most part, when she entered a particular hall or joined a specific club, I could strategically place myself at her walking cross-sections. When she entered my peripheral, the world stopped rotating. From head to toe, she pieced her outfits together like *America's Next Top Model*. To top it off, her honey-dipped complexion and charisma illuminated my soul. *Maybe if she had been in my math class a few years ago, she would have accepted my invitation to be her study partner. Then, we both would have finished that course with flying colors.* Yep, I was smitten, to say the least!

Although Collins Elementary has since been closed due to budgetary cuts and low enrollment, this education facility opened the doors to a delayed but forever love. Our philia love remained a friendly connection for the first few decades. Once I transitioned to high school and moved in with Aunt Mattie, Robernett and I lost contact. Our social circles were no longer intertwined. We graduated from high school with crushes on different beaus. But, given the proximity of every most frequented store and refuge in Augusta, it was only a matter of time before we serendipitously reconnected. As a city with an area of three-hundred-plus square miles, anyone could drive the speed limit and reach the other side of town in less than twenty minutes. In fact, if you leave a particular destination and forget to confirm your arrival, the phone rings would ignite across blocks. My village was keen on keeping tabs on every citizen, especially young adults. Such a golden rule often slipped my mind when I unexpectedly ran into Robernett at the gas pumps or local convenience stores. After offering to pump her gas, I would bid her farewell, hoping and praying I would see her again at Wal-Mart or her place of work, J B White's department store. This dream was not a drastically farfetched hope, as any resident in Augusta crossed paths with the same person every three to six months, like clockwork.

For the next ten years, our professional lives carried us in opposite directions. While I earned a living with law enforcement, Robernett worked at the cosmetic counter at the department store located in the National Hills Shopping Center, in West Augusta, on

Washington Road. Although she sported the company's generic uniform, a white lab coat and professional bottoms, she wore it exquisitely. She naturally fit the perfect prototype for hitting record-breaking perfume sales, a Kodak smile, a beautiful frame, and long, pretty legs. At the very moment I entered her aura, I was instantly captivated. Light floral scents sprinkled with lavender, combined with her reassuring presence, manifested into the highlight of my day. Every season, I patiently waited for the heavens to open and connect our daily commutes.

On a rare occasion, my lieutenant assigned me to patrol the southside of Augusta, Highway Twenty-Five, called Peach Orchard Road, among Augusta natives. Back then, Robernett juggled two jobs, like me: one at Krystal Hamburgers and the other at Sconyers BBQ. Owned and operated by Larry Sconyers, former Augusta Mayor, and his family, this city landmark continues to be famous. Tourists and residents frequented this family-friendly restaurant to indulge in top-of-the-notch barbeque. Sconyers' reputation for conjuring up the best recipes and southern dishes rapidly spread from Georgia to Washington, D.C. In fact, President Jimmy Carter hired Larry Sconyers to cater a Southern meal on the lawn of the White House. Presumably, these two restaurants offered more flexible hours and better tips than the department store. If I missed her at work, it was only a matter of months before I would catch her on the road.

As soon I caught wind of her one and only bright, kelly-green Volkswagen Bug, my world lit up. Once I visually confirmed she was the actual driver commuting alone, I playfully grinned. The pursuit began. I pressed the gas pedal to my Crown Victoria police vehicle and switched on my blue lights. When she caught a glimpse of the flashing lights trailing her, she slowed down. I followed the protocol of a routine traffic stop. We both entered the emergency lane. I excitedly hopped out of the car. As I neared her vehicle, I saw her puzzled face. Her precious hands firmly gripped the steering wheel. I tapped on her window and literally observed her facial expression transform from dire panic to pleasant surprise.

"Osborn! Boy, you scared me!" she said with a trembling voice.

When she uttered my birth name I left behind in elementary school, our childhood love teleported us back to Ursula Collins hallways. Instantly, my juvenile infatuation resurfaced. If there was such a thing as a time machine, this would be it.

I smiled from ear to ear and then stated, "Hey, pretty lady. I just wanted to see you."

"There are plenty of other ways to see me, Oz, and seeing a police car is the last thing I want after working a super long shift," she recanted, blushing and grinning. Boy, did she look a pretty sight!

"I sincerely apologize," I said, removing my cap and placing it over my heart. "I had to place my eyes on you. Take my number and call me some time," I beckoned as I tapped her hood and waved goodbye.

By the third time I pulled her over, I was sure that although her heart may have initially skipped a few beats in the most nightmarish fashion, she had acclimated to my harmless approach. Eventually, she found it audacious, but pleasantly flattering. So, the extent of our interaction was when the stars miraculously aligned, or every three to four years. Whether we bumped into each other or not, I am confident she had some inclination that I was crazy about her. Part of me believed she had a slight crush on me as well. Neither one of us entertained that feeling, as we were married and building our own families. It was not our season just yet. Yet, as always, all would be well in the good Lord's time.

In the meantime, in the early nineties, I had the privilege of joining the Augusta Chapter of the 100 Black Men of America. As an organization, we empowered people to become self-sufficient contributors to the fabric of Augusta's culture. I subscribed to their pillars of education, health, economic development, and leadership. Within this organization, I built relationships with strangers who became lifelong brothers. For example, Clinton McGill moved to metro Atlanta and offered me a place to stay upon arrival. He was a vital bridge that brought me over from one side of the river to another, from a former chapter of my life to a new page.

After serving fifteen consecutive years in law enforcement, protecting, and serving the citizens of my beloved hometown, I was on track to be a sheriff in no time. Then, a massive paradigm shift occurred in my professional and personal world. A career opportunity I cherished incredibly, and appeared to possess upward mobility, suddenly came crashing down. Unfortunately, my youthful marriage tumbled down alongside it. My future hung in the abyss of uncertainty and tested faith. This valley would prove yet another pruning of the vine and cleansing in the fire. When all else falls apart, keeping the faith and one's eyes fixed on God is more vital than ever. Sure, take a glance at problems, but focus on the ensuing promises.

On Duty For Assignments And Social Alignment

Whether charting a new career or navigating a fresh relationship, the bold decision to assume a risk-taker spirit is an unwavering requirement. As the popular adage states, you miss 100% of the shots you do not take. Most people do not fail because they are ill-equipped or uneducated. These individuals miss their blessings and success because they allow fear to stop them from taking the first step. Getting started is a brave gesture and a faithful move to pursue more in life. It is only when a person begins a new venture that they open their world up to greater possibilities.

Working in law enforcement, getting my apartment, and marrying my girlfriend each required a brave step out in faith. There was no roadmap to ensure I succeeded in these areas, but I had the will and determination to put forth my best effort. Previously, I had not watched a family member or close mentor climb the ranks in their respective career. Additionally, I had yet to have a successful marriage exemplar in my immediate reach for which I could model my union. However, I exercised my faith, giving each professional and personal endeavor my best shot. Ironically, each of these experiences ended in time, but the lessons acquired along the journey were invaluable contributors to my personal advancement.

When circumstances stretch you beyond your comfort zone, allow them to reshape your perspective, to strengthen your talents. You never reach your full potential if you avoid unfamiliar pathways. Instead, you spend life twiddling your thumbs or playing a repetitive tune of what-ifs and could-have-beens. These are funeral dirges, my friend. Sing a new song; dance to it, even if everyone is looking. From this point forward, embrace the opportunity to have a series of firsthand experiences that make life worth living. Such novice embarkments turn lessons into lifelong opportunities. Transformation is akin to pressing the fast-forward button on your favorite movie to identify plot twists and discover the end. While it is a natural temptation to want to skip ahead to the conclusion and avoid the pain, it is only through the pain and refinement in the fire that God can do His work in your heart. It is only after these turning points that advantageous growth transpires. Taking risks will pay off. You will read how decisive action also paid off for me. Stay with me on the blessed journey. We have come a long way, but we still have a good way to go.

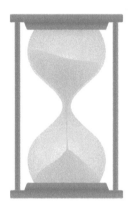

"Two things define you:
Your patience when you
have nothing
and your attitude when you
have everything."

— George Bernard Shaw

Chapter 5
A Road of Detours and Destiny

My final stint in Augusta, Georgia, was marked by employment with an enforcement division I abhorred to the highest degree: the Georgia Department of Corrections. Since no severance check or unemployment benefit was earmarked for my checking account, I chose to grin and bear it. Between earning a meager $9.67 per hour and a few thousand dollars in savings, I could cover rent plus a few necessary utility bills. As a young guy in my early thirties, the psychological impact of being unable to consistently provide the financial support my family direly needed persistently knocked at the door. Hence, I accepted a temporary position in Augusta's state correctional facility and hospital, a restrictive environment fueled by depressive realities and toxic energies.

Augusta State Medical Prison is a multi-purpose facility located in the western part of Richmond County in Grovetown, just fifteen minutes from the Fort Gordon Military base. On one side, it houses offenders requiring physician treatment for medical or mental challenges. Other areas offered well-needed adult education, Bible study, and work activities. Yet the adults had to assume a posture to receive these lifelong benefits. At any moment, it can house over one thousand inmates. For me, aiding and monitoring double amputees and mentally deranged men who mirrored a similar demographic to me over-shadowed my youthful ambition. Being caged up in this building for eight hours inadvertently made me feel locked up too. At any rate, I could not breathe in between such depressing, suffocating walls.

Attending work became progressively arduous as each day passed. At any instant I turned onto Indian Springs Drive, I gasped for oxygen as my heart palpitations increased simultaneously. Body reactions similar to a panic attack echoed my inner thinking. "Oz, God's got something better for you," I tried to remind myself at every laborious turn. However, prevalent financial burdens muted this voice more frequently as I stepped out of my car day after day until the voice went silent altogether. So, I leveraged my paid time off to seize some allotted taste of freedom. One day, I was so emotionally drained that I looked at my uniform, perfectly ironed and hanging in my doorway, then called out sick. I was literally sick and tired of showing up full of energy only to return home in an emotional overdrive, beyond exhausted. I needed time to recharge my engine's batteries instead of haphazardly continuing to just get by on fumes. This was no way to live.

The following week, I was deployed to the correctional academy in Forsyth, Georgia. The Georgia Public Safety Training Center in

Forsyth pioneered an intense officer training program, inclusive of a multitude of field-related courses. Alongside twenty-four other officers in training, I immersed myself in the law enforcement world for four hundred hours. The rigorous curriculum and assessments left little margin for error. Between inmate discipline, legislative law, CPR training, and self-defense tactics, every graduate clearly understood the law was the law. There was little, if any, time for anything else unless it was a lucrative escape, which always lingered in the back of my mind. I fought hard not to succumb to such a counterintuitive, nagging voice's temptation to flee.

Undoubtedly repelled by the idea of becoming a corrections officer, one week before graduation, I invested a few hours perusing the job sections in the *Augusta Chronicle*.

Like William Roberts, a prominent business executive and Grammy-winning rapper popularly known as Rick Ross, I discovered that operating as an unofficial warden in jail was unfulfilling. In the nineties, Ross worked eighteen months in this capacity and quit. As two ambitious men privy to the mistreatment of marginalized groups, this stifling role was a temporary job, not a lifelong career. How anyone could make it a career was beyond me, but I digress. I suppose a brother has got to do what a brother has to do. Babysitting innocent and guilty adults until their court date arrived did not equate to a purpose-driven routine, let alone life. Being in a dangerous and non-empowering environment forty hours a week was asphyxiating: as if I could afford to allow my oxygen deprivation to get more intense. The heightened discomfort and frustration morphed into dominant persuaders. As soon as I caught wind of a better-paying job in

Savannah, Georgia, I leaped at the opening. I refused to wallow in misery.

Established in the mid-1980s and housed on Savannah State University's campus, the Coastal Georgia Center offered graduate students a convenient and economical option for courses, conferences, and study groups. This two-story academic building on College Street opened its doors to scholars attending neighboring colleges, such as Savannah College of Art and Design and Armstrong University as well. In my role as an events facility manager, my job responsibilities were to ensure the smooth flow of collegiate events and authorize individuals' entry. Additionally, from three to eleven p.m., five days a week, I assisted students in troubleshooting any building issues and counseled those needing an immediate faith boost. The latter duty was an added bonus. I am always delighted to share how God made a favorable way out of no way.

Once I checked in with the off-duty police officer I managed, I drove to my apartment, showered, and called home. Given the hour, I generally spoke to my wife. Occasionally Evynn would still be awake. She placed the phone near his ear. He would utter "Dada" and some other comforting gibberish.

"How is Daddy's baby?" I envisioned his smile and legs wiggling around in pure excitement.

Then, my wife and I hopped off the phone. She supported my demanding schedule layered with cross-state assignments. Yet I did not want to miss Evynn's milestones, such as his first step, and couldn't wait to return home.

After this nightly check-in, I laid out my clothes for work and drank a glass of cold milk. This would hold me over until four-thirty the next morning when I would start this painstaking and sacrificial process all over again.

"Welcome to McDonald's." This greeting repeatedly rang in my ear from the second the clock struck five a.m. After a brisk walk from my apartment complex, I started my second job as a maintenance man. Located at the intersection of Eisenhower and Waters Avenues, this fast-food establishment provided the means to cover my rent, automobile, and other paltry needs. It was here my hunger pains were muted with a warm sausage biscuit or egg McMuffin paired with the occasional black coffee. Like my morning charge of Arabica beans, I consistently gravitated to predictable, unfiltered situations and people. After I clocked out at one in the afternoon, I sprinted home and readied myself for my main job at Coastal.

Every two weeks, I earned a steady paycheck and sent it via next-day delivery to my wife back in Augusta. We maintained a consistent, predictable routine for the earlier stages of our short-lived union. Of course, I did not ascertain the brevity of being the working poor. However, looking back, I suppose we could not have found any degree of peace and growth living under those circumstances. Talk about running on fumes and turkey sandwiches!

As you know, the cunning devil loves idle time, but I refused to leave an open hour for his negative interruption to be a possibility. I employed every possible action within my control to be the man who took care of his family, even if it materialized into working fourteen-hour per day. Nothing gave me a greater sense of fulfillment.

Eventually, this unsustainable grind rendered an additional nudge to stop settling and be intentional about my direction in life. One fateful day, our restaurant manager called us to the dining area before our morning shift commenced.

With clipboard and pen in hand, our manager demanded our attention. "Listen, everyone. We are just three days away from our second annual restaurant inspection. Because the Georgia Department of Public Health dinged us a few times on the first audit, it is our duty to ensure we pass this one with flying colors."

The shift manager perused his checklist and began delegating tasks. "Jim, you'll handle the FIFO method with our food. Check the dates and discard expired or nearly expired items first."

Then, he scanned the room and paused. His gaze rested on me, probably the youngest one working this shift, and he handed me a putty knife.

"Oz, we need the floor to be spotless. Scrape off the black grease marks and gum on the floor tiles," he directed.

I gulped and replied, "Yes, sir."

Talk about gut-wrenching shock. Never in a million years did I envision fathom I would find myself on my hands and knees, working to earn an income. I might as well have been in the Army, scrubbing the floor with a toothbrush. Yet, with staggering responsibilities hanging over my head, I swallowed my pride and started cleaning until that floor was clean enough to eat off. As I inched towards the door, looming shadows of two men were cast across the floor. I peered up and saw a pair of police officers entering. I wiped the sweat from my forehead, then mustered up a "Good morning, Officers." *Wow, I remember the respect and honor associated with being a man in uniform. Now I am working in this subservient role.* Yet, in my heart of hearts, I found refuge in knowing God had a bigger plan for my life. Never think you are above any task or person. Humility is an important asset in your growth process.

During my six-month stint in Savannah, Georgia, my mental and physical state started declining as my adrenaline dwindled. My desire to play an active role in my son's upbringing and create more memories with my family became uncontainable. Before a pity party could overcast my problem-solving ability, I phoned my friend, Jeff Annis, in Augusta. Initially, we shared our post-high school life events. Then, Jeff raved about his family's thriving pest control company. Annis Pest Control ranked in the top three businesses in the area and paid handsomely. Sure, this role was way out of my wheelhouse, but I firmly believed I was capable of all things, especially since income was the main culprit creating distance between my family and me. Perhaps it was presumptive of me to assume I could wear any number of hats. However, remember, I subscribed to a Word that underscored my versatility: I can do all things through Christ who strengthens me (Philippians 4:13 NKJV).

Again, after ninety days, either the smell of fumes or termination of bugs forced me to resign. Although I was grateful for this interim opportunity, I ascertained the importance of building something my family could inherit as well, even if it were just a pension. After little Evynn and my wife drifted into a deep slumber that night, I reclined on the sofa and closed my eyes. *Should I return to law enforcement? This comes naturally to me,* I thought. This idea was underscored by the genuine reality that I was a free spirit accustomed to driving around in my patrol car and adding value to my community. Yet my time in that space left a bitter taste in my mouth. I firmly believed all money was not good money. I shut down my thoughts and went into prayer. God would intervene and provide a way.

The timing could not have been better for a newfound opportunity. Fred Pryor's professional training and career development company based in Kansas was in town. When time allowed, I sat in on a few presentations transpiring in one of our breakrooms. Attentively, I took copious notes of informative seminars curated for individuals, teams, and organizations. Given the notable outcomes yielded by completing these trainings, Fortune 500 companies, universities, and business-minded professionals invested in these programs. After the first training concluded, I approached the trainer and introduced myself. Quickly, we built a genuine rapport with each other. This facilitator complimented me. "Young man, you are a well-dressed, polished, sharp man with a distinguished posture of a true leader." He shared minimal insights into any prospective job, but those golden nuggets never escaped my mind.

I could see myself commanding the room's attention and orating best corporate practices too. The imagery was practically euphoric.

Once the seminars concluded, I stayed behind and spoke one-on-one with the lead trainer, Instructor Moore, with just two weeks left. I shared my resume with him and sought his advice on whether I should embrace the Fred Pryor opportunity. I will never forget the look on his face as he stood over me while I was sitting; he said, "Get the hell out of here, but finish this class first!" I rushed to a payphone, dialed the headquarters office of Fred Pryor, and inquired about the next upcoming audition and training program. As agreed, I finished the law enforcement training and never looked back. I purchased a roundtrip ticket to Kansas with my last two paychecks, put my navy-blue Jones-New York Suit in the dry cleaners, and took the best pair of shoes I've ever worn to Fox Shoe Repair downtown on 8th Street to be shined. Although I was under serving, I anticipated filling the shoes of former speakers, like the outstanding Les Brown and Martin Luther King Jr.

At that current time, I had only been on an airplane once since high school. After my class field trip, I mostly traveled in the South, primarily between major cities in Georgia and South Carolina. This was a newfound venture altogether, and I was readily open to the associated possibilities.

As fate would have it, the two separate worlds of Robernett and I collided once again one Sunday afternoon. After enjoying a delicious home-cooked dinner with Aunt Mattie, I cruised back to my apartment. Immediately after unlocking the door of my soon-to-be bachelor pad in Champion Pines, the silence of living alone met me at the entryway. Flooded by a range of emotions coupled with immense boredom, I picked up my keys. I desperately needed to clear my head and not wallow in my current brokenness, so I hopped back in my car and drove up the street to Club Millennium on North Leg Road. This establishment was a smooth club where adult-age singles and couples gathered in preparation for the upcoming week. When I entered, loving partners exchanged heartfelt public displays of affection. I nodded as a wishful gesture that their union would be blissful and eternal. Then, I eyed the first available seat at the bar and awaited the bartender. Thirty minutes elapsed as I sipped on my Crown Royal and Coca-Cola and found contentment in my own company.

Throughout this evening, security continued to check IDs at the door. Then, a familiar voice resounded throughout the atmosphere. It was Robernett standing at the doorway. Immediately, as she gazed across the club towards the bar, we made eye contact. I charismatically waved her over in my direction. As her long legs gracefully glided toward me, I thought, "Well, I'll be damned!" Today must be my lucky day or perhaps a divine blessing at the bar. After all, it was Sunday after church. Mesmerized, I swiftly stood up, greeted her, and pulled out an adjacent chair.

We shared a few cocktails, laughed at the good old times, updated each other on our relationship status, and were just present. Ironically, I shared that I, too, was separated and nearing my divorce settlement. The two of us were each other's listening ear and safe space. Robernett openly conveyed her divorce was approaching its final days. After hearing that disheartening news, our all-time favorite song, "Power of Love" by Grammy Award-winning vocalist Luther Vandross, sounded. The moment seemed like it was meant to be. I extended my hand, then escorted her to the dance floor. We two-stepped and exchanged a few laughs to a soothing backdrop of rhythm and blues. Then, Luther sang, *"Hold me closer and every minute of every hour, feel the power of love, hold me tighter, take me higher, and feel the fire of the power of love."* As I pulled her to my chest, spinning her around like the princess she was, our embrace emitted warmth like a magical place. It was perplexing how any fool could let this lady slip through his fingers like sand.

After sunset, I covered our tab and respectfully walked her outside. We innocently exchanged numbers and genuine hugs. Then, we resolutely drove off into an evolving abyss of our two separate, but similarly fuming worlds. Neither one of us knew external shifts would add an extra layer of pressure to our lives.

On the cusp of a new millennium, the year 2000 marked the turn of a new century and a plausible global shutdown. Millions wondered if technology as we knew it would go up in flames as the infamous Y2K approached. Media outlets and newspapers covered this alleged technological crisis daily. Since I.B.M. and Apple released computers to the mainstream, memories and documents archived on computers over the previous two decades were at risk of total annihilation. Without a backup plan, computer-savvy individuals could watch years of prized digital possessions get lost in the intangible gorge of cyberspace.

To resolve worldwide stressors spreading faster than a California forest fire, one Israeli inventor, Dov Moran, with M-Systems Inc., chose to exercise faith in his creative wit. Moran jumped ahead of the brewing crisis and capitalized on this technology frenzy. Inspired by Toshiba's flash memory invention of the 1980s, Moran created a portable, external hard drive, known as a Disk on Key, physically small enough to fit snugly in your inner coat pocket. Yet space-wise, with an eight-megabyte capacity, a single USB drive provided space for a person's favorite four-minute song or one thousand of their most cherished images. We've certainly come a long way technologically since then!

After Moran filed the first patent for a USB-based P.C. flash disk in April 1999, he fought and won the invention dispute against I.B.M. Meanwhile, consumers flooded big box stores to purchase a few saving devices. Moran's proactive mindset placed him in a wealth-generating space. He capitalized on the anxiousness trickling down from corporate worlds to private abodes. In fact, according to HPCWire, the external memory market was expected to see dollar growth of 25.7% and market price increases for the first time in three years. In 1999 alone, shipments were expected to exceed $3 billion. Nations moved from standstill fear to a newfound faith in technological advancements.

Since I did not own a desktop computer to induce heavy technology reliance, life continued as usual. However, an unsettling urge to reinvent myself emerged. I deemed this societal downswing a clear sign to take immediate action. My focus fixed upon an unceasing sense of urgency to leave my native home ignited within my soul. I bravely decided to feed this burning desire to see where it lit my burgeoning path. After reconfirming my new job with Fred Pryor Training, I was committed to relocating to Atlanta, a melting pot of successful minority enterprisers and a personal jar of favorable outcomes for me. I fathomed dozens of ways this move could take a nosedive into an abyss of trouble. One wrong move and I could wave my dreams farewell. Transplanting to a big city alone meant I would forfeit my beloved support system, who was typically just a phone call or five-minute cruise away.

Sure, Aunt Mattie's friends would welcome me into their robust, nationally spread circle, but I had yet to experience such networking power on my own merit. I would be charged with the hefty task of starting from scratch, independently replanting myself upon new land. But I was inventive and resourceful, trusting that I could handle this task with God as my witness.

Shortly after the sun rose on July 5, I found myself pulling into the Golden Pantry gas station to fill up my 1987 Honda Accord. Two weeks earlier, my dear friends Laurie and Steve, a white couple I met at the Channel 12 TV station, gifted me this vehicle. Unfortunately, the 1996 Grand Cherokee I drove across town conked out a few months prior to my scheduled start date. Although it was an incredible vehicle that commanded attention on the road, I was taking a hefty risk by straying away from my tried and proven Japanese-made automobiles. Talk about running on fumes!

When the cashier placed my change in my sweaty palm, I folded this crisp ten-dollar bill and pushed it to the lowest corner of my right pocket. Since this was the only cash to my name, I guarded this Alexander Hamilton-faced bill like a hawk. I cherished this last ten-dollar bill, placed snugly in the deepest corner of my jean pocket. Even in a place of lack, I was confident in my innate drive to make a dollar out of fifteen cents. Moreover, aiding those within my supportive village gave me an internal sense of abundance. I could always make more money. I'd done it before, and I could do it again.

Since I was a soon-to-be divorcé, I still honored my role as a provider. I paid bills for my soon-to-be ex-wife to care for our two sons, Oz Jr. and Evynn Lamar. Earlier, Aunt Mattie had prepared a big breakfast spread for me that day, including grits, eggs, fried chicken, homemade biscuits, and gravy. It was a meal fit for a young man evolving into an impactful king. I was full of good food and heap loaves of faith.

Peering over my piled clothes, securely insulating my thirteen-inch television, I caught my last glimpse of a billboard promoting the annual Masters Golf Tournament. Yet this tourist season presented a different parallelism. While Tiger Woods was swinging his golf club and reining in millions, I would take a swing at my own championship. I was planting my roots in a new land and determined to establish a winning track record. There was no time for hesitation or second thoughts. I had to strike the iron core of metro Atlanta opportunities while it was hot. Yes, an optimal, big break awaited.

Although petrol filled my payment-free automobile to the brim, emotionally, an all-encompassing emptiness filled me to the metaphorical brim. I was certainly running on fumes. My heartstrings pulled back as I reached the thirty-minute mark. As a man who walked proudly in his capacity to be a provider for his loved ones, I was extremely concerned about Aunt Mattie's welfare during my absence. Sure, she would still coach high school students on obtaining lucrative college offers and play an active role in her Delta Sigma Theta sorority. But I was physically missing in the day-to-day action. For the decade leading up to my departure, Aunt Mattie and I were everything to each other within our family circle. Residents who did not know my family well even assumed she had given birth to me herself. She was truly my second mother.

With all that aside, time was of the essence; my journey commenced. Augusta, Georgia, inclusive of my comfort and roots, was in my rearview mirror. Forging ahead on a long stretch of road ahead, I had a few mustard seeds of faith, ounces of oxytocin, and a music selection of praise. Before apprehension or doubt nestled deeply into my spirit, I quickly shifted gears. I popped Kirk Franklin's Nu Nation CD into the player. As his upbeat and inspirational compilation played, a calming sense of hopeful zeal accompanied me along my two-hour ride. I sensed God seated in the passenger seat, accompanying me on the journey. He'd never left my side.

The Intersection Of Detours And Destiny

Transition does not always mean running for cover, or that danger has abounded. At certain moments, discomfort represents a prime time to establish your upward mobility. When you least expect it, the uncomfortable growth you endure is followed by a timely downpour of blessings. Such pivotal shifts in your personal, emotional, professional, or financial state serve as precursors for self-discovery and a brighter future. The Almighty orchestrates things in a certain way. On multiple occasions, an unexpected, singular shift materialized into my life's most celebrated, bittersweet, life-changing moments. Had the best deacon prophesized that I had a predestined duty to transplant from Augusta to Conyers, I would have responded by asking where on God's green earth Conyers-Rockdale is. Conyers was not a highlighted town in award-winning movies. Despite numerous trips to the notorious Atlanta, I never paid attention to the highway signs that read "Rockdale County."

When it is time to move, signs of assorted sizes and magnitudes will blatantly appear. Little hints may drop on your daily journey. However, if you fail to pay attention to these small but compelling signs, they transform into hardened, gigantic boulders. Once you devise a plan to surmount these blockades, God will strategically throw a spontaneous wrench into your personally orchestrated plan to grab your attention. For me, it was time to move into a different headspace and on to a more divergent career track. Opportunities like these may be the optimal time to move from average living to extraordinary existence. Although it never dawned on me, the Almighty was equipping me for some of my life's greatest challenges and highest rewards all along. Every day I wake up and thank God for my homeland, the bustling city of Augusta, Georgia. It is often only in intentional reflection that our former experiences and the embedded lessons become clear. As the old saying goes, hindsight is twenty-twenty. God replaced my fearful shades with faith-filled lenses, ushering me to see the abundant world He molded in the genesis.

Chapter 6
To Atlanta and Beyond the Global Arena

Big city, Black Mecca of the United States, Atlanta, here I come! Upon settling in at my friend's abode, I repacked and refocused on a different season in adulthood. That Sunday evening, I eagerly flew out to Kansas to complete my onboarding process at Fred Pryor. While the compassionate flight attendant ran down a list of emergency procedures and in-flight best practices, I deeply exhaled. Before my lungs could refill with oxygen, my precautions and speculations ramped up. No, I never second-guessed my ultimate decision to work remotely or finalize my divorce. My current thoughts were based on future outcomes. I pondered, *Would this opportunity be the perfect merger between my current gifts and future aspirations?* Momentarily, I grappled with my choice to leave my familiar career world. Subjugating myself into a newfound professional realm with heightened expectations was risky. By the same token, I trusted the process, finding comfort in my faith-charged battery pack. As my internal voices tussled between the advantages and disadvantages of my chosen journey, the plane took off. Whether I was ready or not, my novel adventure launched too.

Upon landing at the Kansas City International Airport, historical winds of ancestral victories captivated my soul, suffocating any lingering doubt. This Midwest territory, known as a passageway to freedom in northern states, housed various stops for the Underground Railroad. In fact, in 1861, the Kansas Constitution opened habitable land to all people, regardless of their racial and financial background. A decade or two later, Black families founded the town of Nicodemus, named after an enslaved African prince who dutifully purchased his own freedom. Fast forward to 1954, the National Association for the Advancement of Colored People (NAACP) thrust inequitable education experiences and segregation into the limelight, thus initiating the landmark *Brown vs. Board of Education* case in Topeka, Kansas. Such historical trials and triumphs bred a Kansan culture of elevated expectations, visible equality, and groundbreaking career strides. Now, the divine time to exercise similar resilience and determination emerged. The freedom bell sounded for me to secure greater financial and professional liberation. Additionally, my Nesbitt legacy, planted south of the Mason-Dixon line, prominently counted on my success.

Once the airplane buzzed, signaling our safe deboard, I firmly stood in the aisle with invigorated expectancy. School was back in session! After retrieving my luggage from baggage claim, Fred Pryor's executive transportation services picked me up. The driver pulled into the closest three-star hotel, the Red Roof Inn, then I checked in. Whether it was a result of jet lag or pure anticipation, I automatically overlooked the limited amenities in this pet-friendly lodging. Since I regarded this opportunity as a timely blessing, any complaints about company-sponsored housing and meals were futile. After all, a mattress was a bed, just as edible food was a meal. I hungered for bigger, intangible things. Such things would catapult my family from simply surviving to living more abundantly.

At six the next morning, I grabbed a quick granola bar or muffin before rushing to our conference room. Before sunrise, a weeklong intense, rigorous public-speaking training commenced. The following fourteen information-rich hours completely immersed my colleagues and me into the Fred Pryor world. Such sales and oratorical training oriented us to this organization's culture. Each new day presented innovative topics and simulated client projects. For assigned group tasks, we lunched, learned, and strategized like a highly skilled secret society. We constructively poked and prodded until crafted sales pitches were airtight. Role-playing kicked our endorphins into overdrive. From counteracting potential sales objections to sharpening our spoken delivery, each member left more equipped and confident.

Before turning in for the night, we competently presented our projects, paying close attention to precisely regurgitate core principles taught across various sessions. These collaborative experiences exceptionally illustrated how teamwork is deemed a workplace asset. By the eleventh hour, shortly before midnight, I mentally clocked out. Then, I crashed in my hotel room, readying myself for another demanding day. I was dog-tired, but still found this job to be the perfect mixture of answered prayers. Such super-intensive professional training forced me to dig deep and recommit to my greater mission.

This Fred Pryor immersive training presented an opportunity for me to shine. By engaging my natural speaking proclivities for presentational assignments, I won over observant participants, as well as attentive managers. The mere ability to leverage my youth-sprouted oratory skills and showcase them to the team was gratifying beyond measure. Operating within my wheelhouse undoubtedly aided in easing the anxiety associated with entering a demanding sales profession. The art of molding my mind to produce awestruck speeches infused with the underlying need to purchase our products demanded a higher learning curve. At that interval, I pivoted and proficiently coupled my God-given talents with my newly upgraded toolbox. I garnered various tools I could leverage for record-breaking outcomes as I moved forward.

Upon the successful completion of my training evaluation, my adrenaline immediately peaked as I envisioned receiving my first big check within the next fourteen days. Yes, the daily countdown was real. My initial start date fell two weeks before the towering first-of-the-month bills. Due to my irregular employment history leading up to this position, my financial means were bleak. Every bank account was in desperate need of an ample financial infusion like an agricultural county in drought season desires a torrential downpour. Each time I randomly found a quarter on the ground or two nickels to scrape together in my slacks' pocket, I counted it as a blessing. Therefore, before my plane took off to Kansas, I devised a plan to hit the ground running and earn a four-figure check a.s.a.p.

Unfortunately, this company's standard protocol did not align with such a predetermined vision.

On the final day of training, one seasoned coach approached me, shaking my hand. "Congratulations, Oz. The team was astounded by your winning attitude and clever approach this week."

My face warmed with gracious pride. "Thank you, I definitely worked to showcase my ability to garner new clients and move the room."

Nodding her head in agreement, she replied, "Indeed, we are confident you will do just that in time. Although you have completed all the prerequisites with great precision, we typically deploy our new hires in the field after the first ninety days."

What an excruciating gut punch! My heart dropped to the core of my stomach as nervous seat puddles gathered under my arms. Without extended hesitation, I solemnly stated, "Yes, ma'am, I understand."

I quickly concealed my surprise and frustration as I excused myself to the men's room. Looking in the mirror, I thoughtfully confessed, *Lady, I need a ham sandwich a long time before then. I have a wife and children to feed, too. Alright, Oz, time to take control of the situation and control the results that you can.*

As I repacked my suitcase to catch the next flight to Georgia, I cast my cares on the Lord but still vowed to pick up a decent-paying odd job the day I landed. After encountering a few financial trials, I believed in unexpected doors being opened. Yet, one must show up and knock for the floodgates to open. When I returned to my buddy

Clinton McGill's house in Lithonia, a FedEx package was already there with my first assignment, a weeklong tour of the state of Pennsylvania. My second assignment was two weeks in the United Kingdom. *Wow, not only did the company's tenured managers exceed my expectations, but they also trusted my ability to be a leading consultant in the field.* I was beyond ecstatic!

Wheels up, it was time to add to the bottom line. Not only did this first consultant job expand my frequent flyer miles, but it also required an expansion in accessible credit lines. Thankfully, the company always covered business-related expenses, such as air travel, lodging, and vehicle rentals. However, the caveat was that each corporate partner required guests or drivers to swipe their personal credit cards for possible incidental fees. Well, this common procedure posed somewhat of a problem. You see, I only had a whopping $200 limit on my Capital One credit card. As you may know, one single swipe for incidentals maxed out my plastic card instantly until I checked out, and the hold was released. Since the majority of my corporate assignments were at least a weeklong in a faraway city, there was no time to earn additional income with a second job. So, I cashed in on my faith and charisma.

After deboarding, I strolled over to a rental car kiosk like I was walking on water. I greeted the customer service agent, held my breath, and swiped my card. Whew, the machine approved my transaction. This first merchant accepted my card, but there was little wiggle room to cover the weeklong rental fees, lodging holds, and after-work meals. The strong knot in my stomach loosened as the clerk passed me the car keys. Then, I unfolded my written directions, navigating to round two of financial Russian roulette.

As the revolving doors spewed me out into the lobby, droves of guests were simultaneously checking into this four-star hotel, centered at the heart of Chicago. Hence, I anxiously waited to approach the hotel clerk and hear her unpredictable candor. Maybe this next gamble would not obliterate my professional pathway. She motioned me to the counter. Then I handed her my only available card. Swipe! She did a double take and cleared her throat. Next, as if a megaphone dropped into her throat, she clearly announced, "DECLINED." My face heated as sweat beaded along my hairline. I was beyond embarrassed, though, not outdone. Before I could sulk in this unfavorable announcement, I engaged my God-given talent, the genuine gift of gab.

Gifts and talents make up a person's identity, their human capital. Employ them to produce advantageous outcomes. I never shied away from leveraging my effective communication or art of persuasion. Before the hotel clerk could utter another lackluster word, I quickly morphed into the best salesman ever to walk the face of Earth. First, I stepped to the adjacent business center and picked up the courtesy telephone. Then, I boldly marked 1-800-CAPITAL-ONE. Next, with a calm disposition, but equally assertive, professional demeanor, I explained this doomed predicament to the customer service representative. Alongside my brewing humiliation, it seemed as if all inquisitive eyes in the hotel lobby were piercing the back of my head. As I frantically reminded the representative of my consistent payment history, I pleaded for an immediate increase in my credit limit. Like a top-tier real estate agent closing a million-dollar deal, I worked my sales lexicon with magic. Surely, he recognized that failure to approve hotel charges or credit increases would leave me stranded, possibly unemployed, in the windy city. After listening to my desperate narrative, the customer service representative requested to speak with the hotel clerk. Within a quick two-minute discourse, those two made a mutual agreement to my benefit. The hotel clerk handed me the room key. "Mr. Nesbitt, everything has been squared away. You are all set, sir."

Right then, I wanted to jump and shout: "It's a miracle! God extended His favor!" Instead, with my dignity intact, I expressed my gratitude and walked toward the elevators. Within the confines of those four walls, I declared to upgrade my financial credibility and credit accessibility permanently.

Proper planning and budget habits were the wealth commandments I pledged to strictly follow for the next six months. Negotiating and pleading became a well-rehearsed routine. I was no longer embarrassed by an occasional decline, but, more so, I anticipated another beneficial barter with Capital One. I am sure this financial powerhouse kept copious notes on my consistent request for a larger credit limit. With an improved track record, my access increased from $500 to $800, then from $1200 to $2,000. In the interim, I practiced fiscal responsibility on my end by keeping a matching amount of cash in my pocket and my bank account. Then, it dawned on me. I was not asset-poor after all. There was one asset to my name, my note-free car. Thankfully, I owned it outright, with no liens or strings attached. Since I was only in town six to eight days a month, I rarely drove it. With low mileage and great upkeep, it would be appraised well above the average Kelly Blue Book value. Inspired by former signs of fiscal responsibility, I reached into my dresser drawer and proudly clenched the car title. It was time to cash in and buy some more time between paychecks. Yet my naivety in the financial literacy world manifested itself into another back-breaking blow.

Budgeting became a routine practice, but I failed to calculate inflation or unexpected expenses. Funds were undoubtedly tight. That withstanding, I played by the rules, honoring the scripted terms of my legal agreements. On one anomalous week, the fifteenth fell on a holiday weekend. Business transactions were postponed until the following Tuesday. At this inopportune time, the title pawn company reared its snake head and struck at this one-sided advantage. Before leaving my hotel that evening, I phoned my cousin to share my stellar delivery with our potential clients. Listening decision-makers marveled at my training techniques centered around subjects such as quality customer service, supervisory training techniques, and how to talk with tact and skill.

Instantly, he countered this remarkable news with an all-too-familiar, devastating narrative. From his living room window, he narrated the tow truck backing up to my car. Then, an unknown driver hopped out and hitched my vehicle onto their truck. To impede this repossession, he grabbed the cordless phone and rushed to the driveway. He informed the truck operator that I would return to town and that I had the necessary funds. Unfortunately, this contracted driver silently and blatantly ignored these facts. Then, the truck sped off, firing on all cylinders. Any desperate plea for grace was left in the dust.

As soon as the plane landed, I nearly sprinted to the arrival corridor of Atlanta Hartsfield Jackson Airport. I quickly tossed my suitcases in the trunk like a hungry sabertooth tiger was on my heels. Then, my concerned cousin transported me directly to the title company. Stress-induced hyperventilation commenced when I did not see my car parked on their lot. The nonchalant agent reiterated that monthly payments were due on the second Friday of the month, regardless of approved federal holidays. Initially, I thoroughly explained the verbal agreement I had with the original agent and my coinciding payment schedule. Even the bank statement clearly showed the funds were debited from my checking account. Thus, the financial transaction should be posted first thing Tuesday morning. Still, the agent was unmoved by my appeals, which made my blood boil. Still, I cautiously spoke and maintained my composure, never forgetting that I stood as a tall Black man in a new city where contentious police involvement could be sparked at the drop of a dime. My limitless pleas were falling on deaf ears as I fell victim to predatory lending.

Financial predators are similar to opportunistic con artists dressed in sheep's clothing. Much like bloodthirsty sharks, these lenders lurk for the sweat and tears of hardworking Americans trying to keep themselves afloat during financially debilitating tides. Approved small-dollar loans are a vicious antagonist in one's quest to gain their financial footing. Even when employed individuals like me play by the contractual terms, these profit-hungry lenders manage clients according to their own undisclosed rule book. Jovial window promotions and friendly on-boarders target families working diligently to keep their heads above water. Then, with clouded judgment and minimum financial acumen, these unfortunate victims become conquered prey as they sign their assets away. After making hefty payments, such borrowers remain deadlocked in the rat race to get back on their feet. The mere goal of reclaiming any pawned asset is nearly impossible, especially given the ballooning interest rates.

In Georgia alone, car title loans can carry up to 300% interest and tack on additional fees, totaling more than 60% annual percentage rate. This means a person pays for their car ten times plus a few other vehicles before redeeming their car ownership paperwork. Yes, this is ludicrous. Such loan terms maliciously trap thousands of honest workers daily. And I vowed to never be shackled to those manipulative entanglements again.

As I knocked out my global rounds, reaching thirty-three of the fifty states and two weeks in the United Kingdom, I meticulously budgeted my earnings with extreme precision. Between paychecks, I constantly communicated with Capital One and reviewed my checking account balances. My mission was to show lenders I was a faithful payer worthy of accessing substantial amounts of cash. Additionally, creditworthiness was an immutable factor in crafting a financially sound legacy. Contrarily, on opposite ends of the globe, a radical leader constructed a strikingly different idea of legacy. Led by this violent extremist, a foreign group egregiously displayed their religious beliefs and American hatred. Outside of the Tulsa, Oklahoma bombings that obliterated Black businesses and homes, this barbaric attack marked one of the wretched ones on American soil. Comfort, as we knew it, dissolved into thin air like fumes released from a tailpipe. Had our globally recognized country reached the end of the first-world road?

Once again, unforeseen global shifts transpired, producing countless changes beyond my single-handed control. The 9/11 terrorist attack on the United States was a complete game changer. On this particular morning, I was working my part-time job and putting up stock at the local Ingles Grocery store on Highway 20 South, in the Honey Creek area. As hijackers crashed into the Twin Towers, I witnessed our country burn in fumes alongside my burgeoning career. In a panic to insulate my family from brewing financial freezes, I rushed to the closest Regions Bank. While standing in line, a gentleman approached, introducing himself as a key decision-maker in Rockdale County. He asked if I would be interested in a position with the local school district. Looking at my appearance and observing my attitude, he assured me that I would be a good fit. Unsure how our economy would recover, I immediately explored this income-generating offer to shore up my familial obligations.

Coupled with the dot-com bubble, the country's economy took a nosedive. Corporate expansions and quarterly expenditures were at a standstill. Since companies were not hiring consultants in comparison to previous years, adding a third income source to my cash flow was exceptionally wise. Within a week, I landed a position as the In-School Suspension (ISS) Instructor for Rockdale County High School. It perfectly facilitated my ability to combat rising inflation or infrequent contracts. In fact, I only made twelve flights after the 9/11 incident. My final assignment occurred in Knoxville, Tennessee, home to the city's first integrated business, Bijou Theatre. As a law-abiding man, I banked on the positive advantages yielded by integration but never left my life's trajectory in the hands of the powers to be.

Financial commitments are not absolved due to economic recessions or booms. Being a former cop, I knew firsthand the debilitating, life-altering consequences of missing child support payments. I wanted no part of those legal ramifications. Therefore, being the stockman at Ingles was one of my many do-what-you-gotta-do jobs. My main goal was to stay afloat and out of trouble. Hence, you can imagine my huge surprise when handcuffs were placed around my wrists. Did I overlook a parking ticket, or was this a case of mistaken identity? Why was I being arrested and hauled back to Augusta? Then, the officer pulled up the charges: delinquent child support payments. Since my employer automatically deducted this court-mandated amount like clockwork, I was baffled by these bogus legal charges. Here I was, a hardworking Black man in America, being wrongfully accused due to a clerical misstep beyond my control.

Traveling this three-hour bumpy ride along Interstate 20, I profusely worked to counteract my unnerving frustrations. I reflected on the significant milestones I accomplished since leaving my hometown. Then, I patted myself on the back for being an upright man who handled business. The state patrol van pulled into the parking lot. Disheartened and embarrassed to be behind bars in the same facility where I worked, this was a hard pill to swallow, especially because I was undeniably innocent. Fortunately, the Richmond County Jail system employed citizens who recognized me and extended the most incredible level of respect. I am sure this was not their first rodeo with booking a notable leader dragged abruptly into jail without any prior record.

Being blindsided by this legal matter was a permanent reminder to keep my income consistent and my financial matters in order. Thankfully, I had detailed paperwork in order which illustrated, clearly in black and white, that each monthly deduction occurred on or before its due date. The guard unlocked my cell within twenty-four hours, saying I could go. There was no need to prolong my unmerited incarceration since I was only guilty of being consistently resourceful and responsible. After being released, I phoned my long-time friends from my old neighborhood. They kindly transported me back to Conyers. There, I continued to put in overtime and juggle multiple jobs to exceed my financial agreements.

Ironically, the same court system mistakenly calculated my required deductions. Once my boys graduated, the government sent me a refund check because my consistent, timely payments exceeded the court-mandated amounts. Sure, this unstated gesture of apology was soothing, but on a macroscale, there is never a price too high for my sons. God had blessed me to father two fine boys, Oz Jr. and Evynn Lamar. My firstborn, Oz Jr., not only shared my name, but he was also the spitting image of me in every visible way. A mild-mannered version of me with a huge heart, my eldest was a gifted chef like my mother and me. He took to culinary arts at an early age. After being in the Navy, he received his degree in Culinary Arts. My second son, Evynn, embodied my gregarious personality on steroids! Inquisitive, smart, persuasive, and an independent thinker, my youngest pursued a relentless quest for success and family. A Morehouse College graduate working towards his master's degree, Evynn embodies the new era of Nesbitts. From birth, these two outstanding young men have made Mom, Dad, Aunt Mattie, and me extremely proud as they follow in our footsteps while charting a higher level of greatness.

Outside of lifestyle expenses, such as mortgage-related expenditures and monthly child support payments, my family kept fire under my butt to make big things happen. Even during uncertain times, I made a daily commitment to create a secure, stable, safe, and comfortable place for my new wife and daughters as well. A short list of my former workplaces includes Clarion Metals, Kroger, Michelangelo's Italian Restaurant, Old Town Feed Store, a southern-style catfish restaurant, and Applebee's in Stonecrest. Shockingly, I once accepted a "gig" as a movie extra for the Put It on Me Video with Rapper Ja-Rule; I played the role of a cop and made $75 for twelve hours, topped with a free catered lunch. From working three contracted jobs to building relationships with community members, students, parents, and local church folks, I weaved myself into the very fabric of Rockdale County. Without a shadow of a doubt, in the most dignified way, I trusted that God and the three positive A's (attitude, approach, and appearance) were working in my favor. To this very day, my omnipotent provider has kept me.

New Territory And Needed Growth

Blessings come in many forms, not just wrapped in dollar signs. In fact, your pre-ordained talents are the blessed pavers needed for progression, those that can literally part the Red Sea of overdraft accounts and weary souls. Remember, the greatest level of faith and self-belief are demanded when you are on the crux of a major breakthrough. In other words, faith and fear are an ever-present yin and yang, just like the warring voices in my head as I boarded that flight to Kansas years ago. These interconnected forces keep you on your toes during the day and gift you a deep inertia by night. Within frequent immersions into uncomfortable days, tap into your self-belief and inherent skills. Relinquish any self-deprecating acts. Hone in on your strengths. When you face a big decision or dilemma, simply ask yourself these four questions:

1. How big is my why?
2. How do I make my faith bigger than my fear?
3. How bad do I want that better life on the other side of this challenge?
4. How will my life change after I conquer this mountain?

As you will learn, God is always bigger than any mountainous problem; hence, your activated faith is bigger than your dormant fear. In the words of the late great gospel recording artist James Cleveland, known as the King of Gospel, "Where is your faith in God?" Grab it. Activate it. Lean on it. Whether heading to the courtroom or planted in a whirlwind of trouble, tap into your faith. This supernatural belief is the real plug to most significant opportunities, profound solutions, and authentic relationships on this side of Heaven.

"We need to accept

that we won't always make

the right decisions,

that we'll screw up royally

sometimes – understanding that

failure is not the opposite of success,

it's part of success."

—Ariana Huffington

Chapter 7
Spring Forward, Give Back

According to the Annual Report on Philanthropy, during the second decade of the twenty-first century, individuals, bequests, foundations, and corporations donated nearly $500 billion to U.S. charities. Despite a global pandemic, rising inflation, and social inequities, benevolent decision-makers still contributed an exceptionally sizeable percentage to the top three sectors receiving most of these funds — religion, education, and human services. Philanthropic efforts promote the call for people to extend philia love to their fellow brethren, not just through words but also in the visible form of hard-earned dollars. When people give, it creates a rippling effect of community empowerment. Weary souls are resuscitated, and the world's heartbeat is preserved.

Anyone generating a decent amount of cash flow is fully aware that the tax advantages associated with charitable donations are a double win. The inevitable change in warm weather also reflects a heightened sense of urgency for donors as Tax Day, April 15th, quickly approaches each year. Financially conscious and good-hearted individuals certainly do not wait for the winter holidays to write a check to their preferred non-profits. It is refreshing to see their after-tax income fund an ambitious scholar's dream, especially before the exorbitant, brutal fees accompanying the summer solstice and beyond.

Spring symbolizes one of the only two moments when the Earth's axis is pointed at a unique coordinate, which is neither towards nor away from our life-giving sun. This rare positioning gifts us equally with twelve hours of beautiful sunshine and twelve hours of a starlit night, barring clouds. At this unique interval, Mother Nature revives dormant trees, hibernating mammals, and discouraged dreamers alike. This seasonal shift also marks an optimal time for old flames, which embody a range of emotionally driven ambitions, inclusive of personal, financial, and social goals, to be reignited.

April showers may very well bring the finest of flowers and budding people together, both promises of new beginnings. That fateful year, the blessed spring was upon us, which meant my long-awaited annual Bachelor Auction was due to take place at the esteemed Sacred Heart Cultural Arts Center. A plethora of radio stations and newspapers spread the word about this philanthropic event. Proceeds from this yearly fundraiser benefited the non-profit organization I had launched a few years earlier. The Male Room Foundation, Inc. operated as a community outreach organization to teach young boys the pillars of self-esteem and self-discipline, among other important life lessons. Once we recruited a few dozen beneficiaries, we strategically curated events to increase their exposure to opportunities beyond Richmond County.

At the culmination of the vernal equinox, we observed these first days of spring by providing a platform for dreams and romance to flourish. We proudly hosted this grand affair for lovers, donors, and friends to connect for a great cause. Packing the stately facility with three hundred to five hundred hopeful women, each female exhibited expansive excitement to see Augusta's debonair and most eligible bachelors. Bachelorettes with the greatest altruism and biggest pockets were to bid on Richmond County's best, brightest, and becoming bachelors. One winning lady would have a five-star date with the most chivalrous, community-driven gentleman, notably. To make this auspicious event a sure grand slam, I vicariously tossed my name in the hat through my envisioned outcomes. I wholeheartedly hoped that Robernett would honor my initial request by serving as one of my hostesses. However, I only wanted her eyes and internal bid to be for one newly divorced bachelor, namely yours truly, in case I failed to make my point obvious enough. I even entertained the idea of her electing me as her presiding officer, her future head of household. Fine-looking men, screaming ladies, and the who's who of Augusta poured into the center. This prominent occasion was a sold-out concert for the greatest rock or country performance encapsulated under the ornate ceilings of the fabulous Fox Theatre of Atlanta.

From distinguished educators and lawyers to esteemed blue-collar workers and college graduates, inclusive of retirees, we all united to push the barometer for those less likely to succeed. Charity donations allowed us to award $2500 in scholarships to hopeful college-bound students. These participants submitted an essay and needed an average grade point average. The labeled underdog, either due to family dynamics or impoverished circumstances, like me, endured correlating failures and poor grades. Such debilitating conditions made their college admission applications less competitive and their denied acceptance more probable, unfortunately. However, my organization spearheaded an equitable solution to this disheartening and debilitating dilemma. We arduously worked to counteract such blight futures, thus giving these aspiring degree-holders a semblance of hope. Every diligent underdog deserved a chance at fulfilling their grandest dreams, but they had to work for it. That was our core requirement, as we wanted each recipient to understand that nothing in life is free. Everyone must be willing to pay in time or resources as they cash in on their goals. This lifelong lesson seems even more vital in today's culture of "me first," where too many people, sadly, possess a sense of entitlement instead of a strong work ethic.

Subsequent to each triumphant event, I reveled in the sheer beauty of being able to galvanize the elite, most erudite, and most genuine trailblazers, thanking God for allowing the stars and planets to align in everyone's favor. Once the team broke down the tables and ensured the center was in tip-top shape, we shared a celebratory toast but headed in our own respective directions. Yet Robernett and I stayed back, recounting the monumental and comical highlights of that unforgettable night. Have you ever seen two sisters outbid each other and compete for the very same man? It was a perplexing but hilarious sight. Then, we naturally switched the topic to our own family matters.

As we happily revealed a few anecdotes about our evolving children, I observed her infinite love for those two brilliant girls. Before the joyous night concluded, I openly divulged my plans to relocate to the big city of Atlanta all by my lonesome. An abrupt but calming silence then transpired. She wished me well and returned to her respective home as the moon cast its light on her pretty face. Before the light turned green, she flashed one last alluring smile my way. Following that eventful evening, we connected sporadically via telephone for a handful of amicable conversations. Nonetheless, both of us were laser-focused on doing what was in the best interest of our growing families and our personal endeavors.

To shift gears a little, managing an organization and pooling together resources in a city two to three hours from my current abode proved to be quite cumbersome and challenging. I was already working full-time, overtime, and all the time. So, I dissolved my non-profit business a year after leaving Augusta. Yet, I remained a strong proponent of college and community empowerment throughout my native city. I never swayed from my life's calling to exercise my leadership skills while providing citizens with a tangible leader who enjoyed being a devoted husband and father.

Even with achieving notable sales goals and serving my county, there was a missing piece of my life: a soul-rich wife. Multiple years had passed since Robernett and I had connected. Nevertheless, we did meet face to face again seventy-two hours after my birthday on September 29, 2000. Yep, I remember the exact date, as this evening served as the hallmark for our first official date in my bustling hometown. Since Aunt Mattie was my only surviving elder, I consciously returned to Augusta every two weeks unless I placed an additional special occasion on my hectic and packed calendar. Ironically, this third quarter of the year boomed with A-list events. I accepted two invitations: a church event and a birthday celebration. There was just one catch: I yearned for a date, and not just any available female, but one incredibly special lady. Of course, I automatically thought of the best one on this side of Heaven. I phoned Miss Robernett.

"Hi, pretty lady. Do you have any plans for this upcoming weekend?" I inquired with a smooth tone.

"Hello there, Oz. No, not really. The girls will be at their father's place until suppertime on Sunday. So, after a few house chores, I plan to kick my feet up and relax. Maybe open a bottle of wine," she answered. I could hear the quaint smile in her voice.

"I see; well, how about adding a grand time to your agenda? I reserved two spots for two five-star events happening this weekend around the city. Will you do me the honor of being my date?" I proposed, my heart fluttering.

"Of course. What's the dress code for these five-star events? Do I need to go shopping?" she questioned.

"Believe me, anything you wear will impress all lookers," I stated with a slight chuckle. *Only I will get a front-row seat,* I silently bragged in my head.

Then she eagerly replied, "I have the perfect attire in mind. I will be ready when you get here."

"Thank you, Robernett; I can't wait to see you," I responded.

I hung up, ready to jump in the car without delay. These fluttering butterflies were reflective of a guy who had just asked the prettiest girl in school to prom, and she had said yes! Can you believe it?

Once I made the commute from Atlanta to Augusta, I navigated to her new place and picked her up. Boy, was she dazzling as always! Her classy vibe refueled my tank, while her authenticity fertilized my hopes.

Our first stop was the roast for the infamous J. R. Riles hosted by his church, William Memorial Methodist, on 15th Street. As the speakers told jokes and recounted some of his most notable accomplishments, Robernett and I sat in the wooden pews. Her laughter was indeed medicine for my exhausted soul and music to my weary ears. After such comedic relief, we enjoyed a five-course dinner at Carrabba's Italian Restaurant. We shared the rollercoaster events leading up to that moment, making for vulnerable conversation mixed with tearful and comical experiences alike. Before consuming the last bite of our delicious tiramisu dessert, our waiter advised us that the restaurant would close in ten minutes. For a first date, it was going so exceptionally well that we had lost track of time.

Additionally, we erroneously missed the second event on our schedule, Mr. Lynwood Holmes, Pattie Labelle's number-one fan's thirtieth birthday celebration. Since childhood, Lynwood and I had played in the community and supported each other's endeavors. Prior to coming, I warned him I was bringing a hot date and may arrive a little tardy to the party. He also knew Robernett to be a beautiful, classy lady and thoroughly understood my absence. The world-renowned adage that time flies when you are having fun proved to hold its weight in gold that night. That Sunday, I drove back to Atlanta, repacked, and returned to the airport.

Over the next twenty-four months, Robernett and I continued forming a blossoming relationship, even across multiple county lines. Mutual respect and personal sacrifices kept our union brewing with infinite possibilities. I planted legacy-bound seedlings as our budding romance grew. After a demanding work week and a turbulent flight, I landed in Atlanta that one Friday. By the time I reached my apartment, Robernett was also en route from Augusta. Every twenty minutes or so, I peeked through my blinds, highly anticipating my lovely girlfriend's arrival. Against the backdrop of a fall storm and torrential rains, we were committed to spending the weekend together. Now that she finally melted at my baritone, Barry White voice and the smooth woodsy scent of my cologne, it was an opportune time for us to cement our long-distance relationship.

Upon her arrival, I sprinted to the car, wrapping my arms around her. All worries and anxiety dissolved. As I inhaled her sweetly scented soft body, her body molded into mine. Such a genuine embrace was like she was meant to fit there in my arms. Then, I grabbed her suitcase, holding her hand as I escorted her to my apartment door. After settling in and changing into casual loungewear, it was our time to breathe. We intentionally chose to be totally present at that moment. I pulled a blanket from the closet. Together, we set up an impromptu picnic at the foot of my bed. From Chinese takeout to merlot wine, we had a full spread. We made my bedroom into our own secluded park. Even though money was low, and we were both running on fumes, our faith in this divine, timely gathering was dynamically uncontainable. From that day forward, my dream girl transformed into my number-one cheerleader. What an outstanding way to culminate my birth month and begin an embarkment on our lifetime union. I had to be the luckiest guy alive.

Then, one Saturday, an isolated brunch conversation swiftly changed our entire trajectory. After her arrival, we drove to Ruby Tuesday on Highway 138 in Conyers, GA. As we apportioned a newly released appetizer, I noticed she was quieter than usual. *Did those cats from Ruben's store have her tongue?* I restlessly wondered inwardly to lessen the uneasiness created by the awkward silence.

Our favorite garden salad topped with cherry tomatoes and sliced cucumbers arrived. While I consumed a healthy portion, she only took a few small bites. Then, our jovial waitress brought a smoking-hot sirloin steak, cooked medium-rare, just the way she liked it, but she barely ate a morsel.

So, I inquisitively probed, "Hi, lovely, what's going on in that sweet head of yours?"

She took a profoundly deep breath. "You have an apartment here, and I am renting a place in Augusta. We are paying two rent payments on the first of every month, not to mention utilities and travel fees. Why don't we put this thing together?"

Flabbergasted by her proposal but equally delighted, I asked, "Are you serious? I'd love that if you three are ready."

She responded, "Yes, we are ready now, Oz!"

After we returned to my apartment, I turned on her favorite television series, *Law & Order,* and replayed our life-changing conversation. Not only was my stomach full, but I was quite enamored by her courageous proposition. Based on the assertive tone of her delivery, I also realized she was equipped to handle any further questions or objections I may have countered like an attorney on this legal drama show. Fortunately, we were on the same side: no convincing needed. It was a quick open-and-shut case.

That brief but dynamic conversation eclipsed all expectations for that scheduled brunch. Ironically, I frequently entertained the idea of those three precious gems relocating to Conyers, but I also understood this situation's fragility. The two girls, Shana and Stacey, were establishing bonds with classmates in their elementary school and learning from familiar teachers. These daughters would be completely uprooted from their current lives and moved into a different home with Mommy's man. Out of unwavering respect for Robernett and her motherly duties, I held back the urge to consolidate our homes and prepare ourselves for marriage. Yet when my queen voiced her desires, my soul did joyous somersaults.

That following summer, we loaded up a U-Haul and trucked ninety minutes to my place in Rockdale County. With my royal queen, two princesses, and God all present under one roof, I was unstoppable. Here, we would become one happy family in the "come up" together. My childhood fairytale came full circle and in perfect timing. We married in April 2003. I could not have been happier. I wanted to moonwalk across the clouds like Michael Jackson and never come down.

Since then, we have conquered the world, hand in hand, with ups and downs, twists and turns, and from no money to more money;

Robernett has been my treasured ride-or-die chick. She exudes an unmatched level of trust and loyalty. From time to time, my cousin, Shay Roundtree, reminded me that I had dated Robernett the longest; he was correct. Not only is she gorgeous, gifted, and loyal, but she is also committed to hanging in there with me, rain or shine. As a dreamer, I am wise enough to know that it takes a special type of personality to stick and stay with a risk-taker like me. Winning and learning seasons impact the entire family unit.

Our testing valley seasons were short-lived but profoundly tough. I will never forget when we were down to just one vehicle, a 2005 Saturn. Unfortunately, our second car was now in the bank's ownership. This repossession and additional financial constraints tested our faith and agility. Our collective responsibility was to creatively juggle four distinct schedules until I purchased another vehicle. Not an easy feat at all, but hand in hand, we committed to running our race, even if it was on pennies and fumes!

I remember seeing my account hit red and praying for a miracle. Before volunteering at the boys' group home, I grabbed the popcorn maker from the top cabinet. Previously, I had promised these teenagers we would make hot, buttery popcorn on my next visit. To my surprise, I opened the machine, and four crisp one-hundred-dollar bills were inside. I blinked ten times to make sure I was not dreaming. Then I called my wife. She, too, was equally thrilled about this monetary miracle. A tangible answer to countless prayers was in my hands.

Alas, just as my success became her success, we shared our struggles. No one gets anything done by themselves. Robernett always offered a helping hand and stood by me in the storms of life. Neither of us feared hard work; she just handled it more fashionably and calmly.

By this time, Shana and Stacey had maximized their involvement in extracurricular activities. Both girls channeled their optimistic energy and became high-spirited cheerleaders. Then, Shana joined the step team and Marine JROTC, a daughter's interest after my own heart. Our demanding schedules operated in full rotation three times a week and on most weekends. When you run on a jammed-packed schedule, there is little time to sit with your problems. It is imperative that you find a way out of no way. Robernett and I did just that as we collectively nurtured our children's interests. While she covered the exorbitant fees associated with school activities and sports, I oversaw the household expenses, plus the monetary expectations of caring for our two boys living in separate cities. Against all odds, we both consistently showed up for our heirs as much as possible. This ongoing arduous task was worth every bead of sweat and tears, plus the dimes and nickels.

Our work-life balance was null and void. I remember Robernett getting off work at three in the afternoon at Piedmont Hospital. Then, she drove five minutes to Rockdale County High School to pick me up unless I coached basketball that evening. Being a phlebotomist, I presumed she was beyond ready to get home to shower off her workday, then maybe find small, blessed moments to refuel. Occasionally, we scooped the girls up from their after-school practices or rehearsals immediately after I jumped in the car. It was a heavy load for me to carry, but I managed. As you can well imagine, the stress, pressure, and tension were higher on some days than others. Although we ran on pure fumes after a hectic week, we routinely mustered up the necessary energy to attend Clifton United Methodist Church as a family every Sunday. That was a commitment to God Almighty I would not forsake. No excuses. I can only hope that Robernett and I instilled the same importance of showing up to serve the Lord in our children by living out our predestined purposes.

Before nightfall, I led our household in communal prayer. Occasionally, after everyone was asleep, I would re-enter a darkened kitchen, sit at the table, rest my elbows on the surface, bury my face in my hands, and release a torrent of tears. These profuse teardrops were a mixture of unbound gratitude and nervous exhaustion. My parents were gone, and I refused to weigh Aunt Mattie down with my adult troubles, so I got Jesus on the main line. After finding solace and recharging my faith battery, I took power walks around the neighborhood. Such a combination proved to be quite the therapeutic combination. Being able to take in fresh air and clear my mind affords me a unique space to find stillness. Outside is the perfect place to walk in isolation and tune in to God's voice, away from calamity and all external forces.

During these meditative escapes, I gathered my thoughts and cried out to God, both in gratitude and in request, all while improving my cardiovascular health. After setting the tone, usually in a forty-five-minute interval, I garner a better understanding of who I need to call and what I need to do to move my success pendulum. To this day, I engage in this therapeutic activity each morning at five while power walking for three miles. I re-enter my abode with tremendous mental, spiritual, and physical fortitude, ready to conquer whatever the day at hand brings.

Moving Forward And Forming Partnerships

Robernett and I are two imperfect people who decided to build our version of real love on a solid foundation of faith, trust, and support. Individually, she illuminates my darkest flaws and challenges me to be a better man, husband, father, and leader. Not only does she anchor me, but she also stretches my faith and self-belief. From my point of view, I am forever her number-one fan. Collectively, in cultivating this daily experience, we vowed always to be authentic and forgiving. There are far too many stories to share in this chapter alone, but one thing I know for sure is that we are unbreakable when tethered together. Not only us, of course; after all, as the Bible says, a threefold cord is not easily broken. When we voluntarily took our vows, we did so seriously and with God as our witness; till death do us part.

Trust, respect, and loyalty must be the main ingredients for any long-lasting relationship recipe. These values and acts grow more profound over time, fomenting unconditional love. For example, I knew, without any doubt, that when the going got tough, Robernett would strap in to stay by my side. Hence, because of her untarnished loyalty, I could comfortably take risks to put our family in a better position. Such devoted acts cemented the necessary building blocks for philia love to transcend to agape love, the kind that God gives and asks us to extend to our fellow brothers and sisters. True love emerges after the initial, temporary lust ends and an intimate friendship takes shape. Love is a much stronger emotion and proverbial act of kindness infused with forgiveness. With a God-fearing love at the helm, a relationship takes on a newfound depth within the construct of submission, whether on calm or stormy waters. We steer that ship together in every season.

Although usually associated with negative connotations, submission ingeniously creates a safe space for trust and loyalty, just as equal portions of trust and loyalty increase each partner's ability to submit to one another entirely. While both of my former wives operated as phenomenal mothers to our sons, our divergent perspectives on partnerships led to divorce. My first marriage was to a sweet young lady. It was short-lived due to our youthful naivety and overbearing parents. Before we could resolve our spats, the in-laws jumped in to offer their subjective opinions. Of course, this only magnified the issues, causing a bigger divide between us. Other divisive elements for marital unions reared their head in my second marriage. We were two strong-willed, ambitious spouses working to coexist and evolve into our better selves. Yet neither of us was willing to surrender power or make certain sacrifices. Eventually, this equated to inner-household competitiveness and disgruntlement.

Through these past experiences and my current role as husband, I learned that matrimony is a constant exchange of give and take. Such actions catapult the strength of unconditional love and legacy-building. There is no fifty-fifty reality. Competition should only exist with the outside world. More importantly, the art of being generously supportive, like Robernett, is a surefire way to increase the sustainability of a lifetime union. Keep God in your marriage and others, especially disgruntled family members, out of your business. Love never fails; it is everlasting. Let your marriage truly be of the First Corinthians kind, not just a Bible reading at your wedding. It is the mosaic of collaborative growth, cross-country travels, and conquerable challenges that come after the marriage ceremony day that matters.

Whether single or married, you too may face similar financial and credit turmoil. Do not make excuses or throw pity parties. Be willing to do whatever it takes to be successful. Surround yourself with an elite circle of people who give constructive criticism from a place of genuine concern. This group shall embrace your dream, challenge your vision, and be your raving fans, whether you win or lose. The resulting synergy among this collective should mirror a peaceful sense of belonging and reassurance. Life will show you the few outliers who will withstand the test of time and remain in your corner. But rest assured, my friend, God is always at your side. Whether married or single, your victorious season is now.

Chapter 8
The Underdog Takes Office

The southeastern corner of the United States is the land of the free and home of the brave, but it is not without toxic chains of pre-biases and anti-integration perspectives. There is Georgia; then there is metro Atlanta. These locations are like the proverbial night and day. In fact, it was not until 1977 that the state's capital elected the first African American mayor of Atlanta, Maynard Jackson. Georgia has voted and been classified as a red state for decades. A few anomalies to these concrete results occurred in 1992 when President Bill Clinton was the Democratic party nominee. The most historical one was in 2004 when Stacey Abrams fought tooth and nail to register over 800,000 citizens. Such an astronomical turnout placed President Joe Biden and Vice President Kamala Harris in office. As racial divides lessened, the opportunity for leaders of color to scale the governmental hierarchy became more tangible.

According to the United States Census Bureau, Rockdale County, Georgia, operates as the home to nearly 96,000 citizens, of which seventy percent are of legal voting age. This bustling county is a diverse mosaic of Blacks, Hispanics, Asians, whites, as well as other groups. Such diversity required an all-inclusive and well-developed strategy to reach eligible voters within a twelve-month span. Outside of basic marketing strategies, we crafted a grassroots plan that met the old-school and new-school voters where they were. From Gen Z and millennials' affinity for social media to Gen X and the baby boomers' gravitation to yard signs, we worked the campaign from every angle.

The campaign season was my regional Super Bowl, but with twelve months for game time, four seasons instead of four quarters. Our political kickoff commenced. We mapped out monthly activities where I could reach a diverse population across the entire county, not just a certain precinct or city. While I shook hands and communicated my vision for Rockdale County, my amazing team secured endorsements, organized fundraisers, and survived on precious few hours of sleep and liters of coffee.

The legacy I set out to craft for my political career was to be the tangible candidate who rolled up my sleeves and presented a holistic, progressive, all-inclusive vision for each citizen. I wanted the people to know I valued them at the individual level. I campaigned every waking hour, which averages eighteen hours a day. Even when I power walked before sunrise, I spoke life and affirmations over my personal duties and county role. Then I thoroughly showered away all the grime and sweat and suited up to look my finest for the day at hand. By eight in the morning, whether light or dark, rain or shine, I was executing the duties as Chairman of Rockdale. Then, once the five o'clock rush hour commenced, I engaged my blessed and much-needed second wind, sometimes caffeine charged by my occasional Starbucks cinnamon latte (sometimes with an extra shot of espresso). Then I was off to the races until the moon shined brightly around nine. From a prospective government official to a campaign manager and everyone in between, every living being needs sufficient hours of shuteye. As the black sky and moon merged, it reminded me that I was still running in a state well below the Mason-Dixon Line.

While I set out to knock on every door, I was fully aware that I was competing against the false narratives perpetuated by the racial divides of the Old South. It is crazy how lies and fear can still live on decades after the civil rights movement of the 1960s, but such is the reality of life. Minds can be a rigid device to alter. This truth resonated in my mind as I approached driveways lined with Confederate flags. Two options surfaced; assume the person is a racist ready to point a shotgun at my head or give the resident a chance to show me the person behind the flag. I chose the latter, relying on God and my better nature to give them the benefit of the doubt with a little grace. Since I am a church boy by nature, building partnerships with the local clergy and God-fearing citizens is nearly automatic. In this light, I found that my natural tendency to seamlessly connect church and state was deemed a winning art by people of faith. The plausible racial tension I encountered on some days and missed on others was a part of my strong commitment to home visits. The great news was that I allowed any hatred I faced to reflect the person's fear of change instead of a deduction in who I was and to see beyond the color of a man's skin. Such home visits were insulated by the three hundred-plus churches I had the privilege of visiting. Here, spiritual upliftment by the Holy Spirit recharged and engulfed me.

After reviewing the polling numbers, my campaign team and I were pleasantly surprised to find that a substantial percentage of local Republicans consistently elected Oz on their ballots for four consecutive terms thus far. Sure, their physical eye inevitably saw skin color and lingering biases, yet the sustainability of their home value and financial pockets spoke greater volumes, much to my benefit. For this segment of swing voters, it was more important to place an accessible and hardworking person in the office. Of course, I was beyond grateful that they realized I met all the written qualifications.

While national leaders may have shunned my method of exceeding such expectations, I bravely and boldly continued to do it, whether by knocking on doors or speaking on radio stations. Imagine the phone calls I received when I ran a campaign advertisement on the radio which announced my personal seven digits. To date, three out of five Rockdale County citizens can access me ninety percent of the time. That is how serious and sincere I am being reachable. This accessibility would be nearly impossible if I used a county-issued telephone number and only worked five days a week during regular business hours. Heck, I have not even committed that number to memory to distribute it at a whim.

Person to person, human to human, my voters and I were alike in that we shared a common vision for Rockdale County. We desired better educational, familial, and economic outcomes for each of the fifteen zip codes and the ten cities within our area. Just as I consciously tried to refrain from discriminating between Republicans and Democrats when voting on the local level, these hardworking citizens refused to do so as well. For tax-paying voters, the right person for the job was the candidate who took swift action while operating with a spirit of integrity, honesty, and loyalty. If a sizable pothole posed a constant danger on our roads driven during morning commutes to work and evening commutes home, these tax-paying drivers and cyclists intuitively held a proper concrete fix over an exorbitant repair bill. Since county budgets incorporated line items for street conditions, it made more sense for these voters to put their predetermined dollars to work instead of their disposable income. Remember, a pair of new tires with installation could be anywhere from four hundred to one thousand dollars, depending on the make and model of a vehicle. Hence, their voting habits favored the commissioner who made popular city routes and the everyday citizens' countywide experience his top priority.

The ever-growing team of the raving #teamoz on social media platforms is the tangible result of my efforts in knocking on doors, visiting churches, partnering with schools, building business partnerships, hosting community events, and being present in every crevice and corner of Rockdale. Finding pockets of people to inform, regardless of race, religion, or ethnicity, proved right and quite advantageous to all involved. This personal pursuit begs the question of why any candidate thinks they can run a campaign behind the scenes or on a television screen alone when there are much better, more practical, and personal remedies. Serving in a political role requires candidates to arduously invest their blood, sweat, and tears. Such amassed equity expands their reach beyond their little box. Potential allies want to witness your visceral hunger for their vote in action. I know without a shadow of a doubt that voting is a privilege. The vote itself is a precious commodity that a person should never underestimate or take for granted.

During my first eight years of public service, I boldly attempted to do it all — I mean everything under the sun, trying to be everything to all people. This overzealous pursuit required me to fulfill various roles: a sales director, a husband, a father, a commissioner, a friend, a mentor, and an active church member. As a precocious child, I watched my mother and Aunt Mattie wear several hats, so I confidently entertained my ability to juggle several roles seamlessly. Each one centered around one consistent act of service, which I became adept at delivering.

In my government role as County Commissioner, I fulfilled the many responsibilities attached to my title. Most weeks, I went over and beyond and amassed a forty-hour investment into bringing even more value to the citizens. Since the role only paid a part-time salary, I could not sacrifice the burgeoning sales career funding my lifestyle. Fortunately, due to hard work and dedication, I established a long-term work history of twelve years with the oldest largest car dealership in the state of GA, which provided me with a flexible schedule, especially when I needed it. Since I was elected as Commissioner, I dutifully fulfilled my weekly obligations. Every Tuesday, rain or shine, hell or high water, my full-time commitment was operating in the capacity of local county commissioner. Of course, this dealership saw a huge benefit in having a Rockdale official on their workforce, as it provided a win-win situation. Whether completing a six-day work week at the car lot or a county obligation, Sundays proved to be the only weekday I put pounding the pavement and working towards a milestone on the back burner. My sabbath was the blessed day to recharge my batteries with my brothers and sisters in Christ in the house of God. All that aside, there was a deficit in this weekly routine, community empowerment.

Shortly after mastering my time allocation, the opportune time came to reignite the service aspect I birthed and mastered in Augusta, GA. God positioned me to amplify my civic duty in the networking arena once again. I mapped out a plan to build an organization comprised of local business owners and entrepreneurs. I titled it The Atlanta Social Networking Alliance. Competing organizations, such as the Commerce Club, targeted established businesses with a track record of profits and scaling. Yet my organization would tap into a pool of newly established organizations and seasoned businesses, thus presenting a complete offering of services and products each member would need in a month's time.

Since we opted not to charge a $250 membership fee similar to existing networking groups, we vowed to support each other's businesses by trading and bartering. For example, if Chris sold wine, she may offer Lynn a case for a discounted rate. In exchange, Lynn would offer Chris a comparable discount on her signs. We were a united front, building wealth simultaneously as we practiced the art of group economics. It was an exceptionally beautiful merger.

At the core of ASNA were three strong-hearted and committed visionaries, Chris Milner, Tiffany Smith, and Jessica Ivey. Chris operated a boutique wine shop called Dogwood Wine and Spirits, located on Dogwood Drive across from Walmart. Her company sourced the richest, most full-bodied red and white wines sourced from vineyards in California to Argentina. After a long workday, I frequented her boutique wine shop to experience a quick immersion in Italian vineyards. Occasionally, Chris provided an educational concierge service to first-time wine drinkers. Learning how to pair beverages with food was much like pairing the right business partners in a new groundbreaking venture.

Tiffany and Jessica were co-owners of Acceptance Insurance on Highway 138 in Conyers. To get their business off the ground, these two went door to door, introducing themselves to everyone within a thirty-mile radius. As fate would have it, these two dedicated professionals pulled our company door one day. Their tenacious energy resonated as if they had been cranking out goals since the break of dawn. Upon entering our Sons' Suzuki dealership, I greeted these two women with a warm welcome and openly listened to their sales pitch. While intently listening to the insurance product offerings in their box, I noticed an equally beneficial proposition: whenever I closed a car sale, I would slide my clients their insurance cards. In return, they would send their clients to my dealership when they expressed interest in buying a new vehicle. I added their business card to my five hundred-plus collection nestled neatly in my home closet.

Proceeding with this surprise interaction to operate as a master networker, I resumed my faithful morning ritual at the dealership. Since the dealership opened at nine sharp, I arrived two hours early to establish my momentum. From sending follow-up emails to calling prospective clients, I created a steady pipeline of viable opportunities. I made sure to keep myself well-fueled with those venti Starbucks cinnamon lattes or freshly brewed black coffee from home. By the time our regularly scheduled sales meeting kicked off, I already had seventy to eighty cards ready to run through the stamp machine. This exceeded the thirty-card minimum. I was on a serious mission to double my commission sales. I calculated the input and output from my hardworking efforts. If I mailed 100 invitations or made 100 calls within forty-eight hours, then I would sell five cars before the week's end.

On this particular evening, the four of us scheduled a meeting to craft the vision and mission for our organization. Our chemistry radiated with mutual comradery, boldness, courage, and execution. We employed a grassroots campaign, then began our recruitment process. Since there were no associated membership dues, each member was responsible for being a valuable contributor to the greater good of each person in the alliance. We started off with a dozen and grew our group to eighty citizens from Rockdale, Dekalb, and Newton Counties. Although this alliance dissolved as we all pursued our own ventures and started our respective families, those established friendships remain strong to this day. Collectively, Chris, Tiffany, and Jessica forged a female trio that manifested into my permanent tribe, fueling my drive to the next level in the government and corporate worlds. To this day, these three powerhouses continue to be day one. They push me to greater heights. I am forever indebted to them. Their love and dedication are truly precious commodities in this day and age of fleeting, shallow friendships in a broken world.

Of this organization, Chris volunteered to be my first campaign treasurer, before we even had enough funds to keep the lights and heat on. Then, when her business suddenly took off, she introduced me to a sharp young man named Andrew (Drew) Bostic. A recent graduate of the University of Georgia, Bostic was a cool-headed numbers man who could run circles around the best-rated certified public accountant. At the time, he was trying his hand at politics and running against Randall Magnum. Bostic's bright energy and intelligence captured the attention of potential voters. Although he did not win the state representative seat, he continued to demonstrate an affinity for government. In a few short months, he transformed into a #teamoz supporter and consistently donated his time, talent, and energy. This guy was as smart as a whip and as sharp as a knife. He illustrated his ability to flip a non-Oz supporter to a die-hard believer and a dilapidated home into a profit-generating asset. Yes, he really was that good. I was pleasantly floored by his high level of integrity, drive, and business acumen. Even with multiple goals in full swing, Bostic never demonstrated a hostile, over-stretched person. When life presented mounting demands at one time, he assessed and prioritized without skipping a beat. Given this agility, he now operates at full speed in a part-time capacity ahead of the next campaign season.

Currently, Bostic is the only paid employee who reports to me monthly. From submitting disclosures to meeting the secretary of state deadlines, he ensures the campaign continues to run lean by the ever-changing law. He is like my little brother and financial consultant wrapped into one dynamic leader. I could not ask for a better, more dedicated bulldog in my corner. On any given day, I am confident that this good brother has my back through thick and thin.

Campaigns And Decisions

Although cliché in nature, the decision to never judge a book by its cover remains wise, tested, and true. Too often, people assess a person's outward appearance, whether it be their clothing, weight, house décor, wealth, where they live, or another physical feature, and draw a flawed conclusion on who the person is at their core. It is a sad but true reality of the harsh world. Remember that the Bible says that while man may look at outward appearances, God looks at the heart. The process of judging a person by appearances or what they have or do not have is a lazy man's way of making assumptions. In the same breath, the person passing unfair judgment forfeits a plausible blessing in disguise. Imagine, for a moment, if a narrow-minded passerby judged every hole in a restaurant's walls and the grimy floors as signs of a sub-par diner; how many people would have a limited palate and an empty stomach?

Learn to value a book not because of its existing cover, but the person's story behind it. There are pages upon pages of stories rich with lessons and wisdom regardless of their title and background. Being judgmental is a natural tendency, but those initial assumptions should not overshadow a person's ability to get to know someone for the true essence of who they are: a child of the Most High. The most unlikely and the most unqualified can be called for a groundbreaking, culture-shifting cause according to His perfect timing. I serve a God who will go into the uttermost darkest, most broken parts of Earth to bring the most far-fetched outcomes to pass. Think of how many applauded biblical figures were the least and the lost among the very ones Jesus came to redeem. Moses did not want to address Pharoah and feared public speaking. David committed adultery and had Bathsheba's husband murdered. Jonah did not want to bring God's good news of grace to the people of Nineveh, judging them to be unworthy. Sarah laughed with disbelief when God told her she would become pregnant at age ninety. Gideon doubted God's ability to raise an army that could defeat the enemy. Jeremiah thought he was too young and inexperienced to be a prophet. Peter denied Jesus as our Lord and Savior was on the cross. Paul was once Saul, a persecutor of the early church followers, and watched as Stephen was stoned for his faith in Christ. Only Jesus was, is, and will be perfect, the unblemished Lamb of God. But my point is that God frequently uses imperfect people to carry out His perfect plans.

On many occasions, I met a sizable number of the folks on the campaign trails while visiting the churches. I also ran into these same people on the "night train," our adult-only club circuit. Outside of politicians and athletes, churchgoers are one of the most judged groups. Door to door, church to church, including the white churches and the nightclubs, I encountered amazing people of faith from all walks of life. Their authentic spirit and collective vision were priceless, a true asset. Yet, like me, these multidimensional believers may love Marvin Gaye's tunes and Kirk Franklin's gospels.

The local clergy was partially responsible for my successful campaigns. With open hearts, without paying attention to my circulating mugshot, God-fearing citizens welcomed me into their churches. We fellowshipped and broke bread together while verbalizing deeply hearted prayers for our community stakeholders. It is vital people meet people where they are, both in physical domains and mental maturity. If they come across your path, it is by divine intervention. This simple encounter can be the pre-orchestrated light to their darkness. Be a good Samaritan to your fellow brother or sister. See how God blesses the harvest.

According to Steven Covey, author of *The Seven Habits of Highly Effective People*, within seven seconds, a person develops eleven distinct impressions or assumptions about a new acquaintance. A good rule of practice to ensure your peace of mind and progress is to refrain from making assumptions about anyone or anything at first sight. Refrain from making snap judgments and immediate disconnect. Give people the benefit of doubt without constraining your perspective by preconceived notions. Assumptions are a lethal interrupter of communication and progress. To that end, the news underscores how unrealistic it is to have an unflawed person running any political office.

NEVER ASSUME ANYTHING. Take nothing and nobody for granted.

"You cannot control what happens to you,
but you can control your attitude
toward what happens to you,
and in that,
you will be
mastering change
rather than allowing it
to master you."

– Brian Tracy

Chapter 9
Go for Human, not Superhero

O ver the next decade, the devastating financial crisis of 2008 continued to place the world in a consistent uproar, and rightfully so. Like the housing market, retirement dollars, college funds, and other investments went up in smoke. To combat these unpredictable losses, families fought tooth and nail to regain some semblance of their designed and normal lives, ones they had grown accustomed to for so long. On the one hand, certain individuals masked their fears and frustration by bravely attempting to continue life unscathed. Contrarily, others embraced an unfortunate, daunting reality by seeking monetary lifelines, in the hopes of rebuilding a better tomorrow. Multi-year financial bailouts for Fortune 500 companies down to everyday working citizens shook the global economy like the catastrophic earthquake in Haiti in January of 2010, leaving unspeakable and unfathomable damage and devastation in its wake that would have far-reaching consequences.

Banks, corporations, small businesses, homeowners, and families alike lamentably tapped into available government assistance while arduously working to keep their heads barely above water. Survival mode cast a dark shadow on dreamers and doers, both near and far, across all demographics. No one was invincible or spared the heartache and headache. For the one percent in higher income tax brackets, the immediate cash flow supplemented their existing assets, facilitating the likelihood for them to sustain their lavish lifestyles. Yet, on the opposite end of the heavily out-of-proportion spectrum, the other ninety-nine percent of the population received smaller amounts of funding allocated to that other ninety-nine percent of the population arduously working to survive. These strikingly different approaches to coping with burnout morphed into an even further divided nation. Yet there were commonalities across chosen past times.

In developed countries, select citizens opted to capitalize on their unemployment spouts and maximize their leisure time. While it was undoubtedly easier to focus on their checking account inching closer to the alarming overdraft line, they refocused on creating long-lasting memories unable to be erased by future catastrophes. This coping mechanism meant scheduling weekday outings at local cinemas, fully capitalizing on the special pricing for matinee hours. Viewers scraped pennies together or tapped into their savings accounts to secure tickets.

Marvel Studios released a box-office hit to deliver an ounce of hope and encourage viewers to unleash their supernatural gifts. The Academy-Award-winning film Iron Man II hit movie theaters worldwide and serendipitously just in the nick of time. Although the methodology used to fund this action-packed movie varied, each person readied themselves in the theater for an attention-grabbing, combat screenplay. It grossed over six hundred million dollars. Robert Downey Jr, Don Cheadle, and a host of other Hollywood stars more than delivered. The plot alone painted a harsh reality that even with a billion-dollar net worth and armored superhero strength, an ambitious man working around the clock leads to catastrophic outcomes. Such an audacious human encountering declining health in tandem with consistent, even unrealistic demands will eventually crash and burn. In May of 2010, my feet were put to the fire, underscoring the reality that I, too, am a human under construction. Talk about a dose of humility!

God captured my attention again that fateful May in spring when He interrupted my grueling grind. He chose this month to teach me a life lesson about the dangers of not nurturing the man in the mirror, me, by unplugging and recharging as needed. Although my energy tank fell well below E, I placed my ambitious drive into full gear. I maintained a full plate of obligations and responsibilities. Juggling my part-time position for eight years required a full-time commitment to Rockdale County. My original dedication never wavered, but I eventually shifted into a laborious autopilot. Building a demanding schedule that included this role and my bread-winning role of working full-time at the dealership manifested into unsustainable overdrive. Emotional stressors and financial worries lurked around in the most profound depths. Yet, as a leading male figure, I put on the strong, gleaming armor of God and bit the bullet.

Serving a dual capacity proved quite commanding, but initially, I skillfully managed the obligations of three people simultaneously: a high-producing sales manager, a tangible Commissioner, and a head of household, much like a living superhero. I found extraordinary pride in waking up fully when the reality was that I was on fumes, going and going, without stopping to refuel properly. I refused to lighten my load, attacking each day with a vengeance. I was making history. But what happens when essential nighttime recharging falls short? The person runs out of luck, gas, and reason. He literally and figuratively breaks down like a car out of gas along the side of the road.

On one Monday evening, my beloved wife and I drove home while conversing about a trivial topic. For an unknown reason, we expressed opposite perspectives. We stubbornly stood our ground. In the back of my mind, I sensed I was too exhausted to channel my natural ability to communicate effectively. Yet I tried to articulate my stance, knowing it was a cardinal sin for couples to go to bed angry at their soulmates. Our tones escalated. A casual conversation that initiated with a simple question morphed into a heated disagreement. Our car filled with incomprehensible noise as if a family of ten were fervently clashing pots and pans together but without any musical skills. There was no undertone of empathy and understanding in sight. Disharmony escalated. I was beyond furious. Surprisingly, steam was not shooting from my ears! Without pausing to de-escalate the situation, I balled up my fist and hit the front windshield like an unknown madman. My wife gasped for air in shocking disbelief as the glass cracked. The sheriff's office was called. Within thirty minutes, I was detained in handcuffs. The next four hours were painstakingly gruesome. Talk about foolish action and an unforgettable moment.

Walking into the Rockdale County Jail, I dropped my head in remorse and embarrassment. This was the second misunderstanding that resulted in my untimely detention, and I was flabbergasted. Then, I peered into the eyes of the suited staff and escaped into an undesirable time capsule. While the young deputy rolled my thumb across the fingerprint ink, I teleported to my early twenties and recalled this intake task being one of my job duties. Holding my inmate number across my chest, I stepped back against the wall. Flash, I realized my heat-of-the-moment reaction carried the potential to interrupt my life with augmented setbacks. As my image entered the national database and my story hit major news lines, immense regret settled in the pit of my stomach like a boulder. The station itself did not pose any danger or added stress. Hats off to the Rockdale Sheriff's Office, who ensured my short stay was as comfortable as possible by placing me in a holding cell away from the general population. The good Lord knows that the latter environment could have caused an uncontainable grenade of mental, spiritual, and physical warfare. I counted my blessings where I could find them.

For four hours, I sat in the Rockdale County Jail, replaying the events of that tumultuous evening. Humiliation consumed my spirit as I gazed into the eyes of my plausible voters, admitting incoming, innocent-until-proven-guilty people. I kicked myself for not choosing to leave the car. Now, here I was, the elected Commissioner who advocates for public safety and correctional facilities, locked up behind bars. My internal voice chastised me, *What the hell are you doing here? What have you done?* That voice was enough for the judge and jury to convict me as "guilty." Just as quickly as I could escape that round of self-inflicted agony, I witnessed years of hard work dangling before me on a fraying thread that was quickly unraveling. Who would I call?

At one of my lowest points, a void resurfaced. Once again, there was no parent or elder to fall back on. I would do anything just to hear the voice of my parents saying, "Baby, it's gonna be alright." There is something that resonates deep in the soul can bring a man to tears or his knees when a mother, grandmother, or someone like my dear Aunt Mattie speaks. Such orated melodies soothe souls and calm internal storms. Not only was this untimely incarceration reflective, but also progressive. Once I finished beating myself up, wishing I could call my angels in Heaven, I adjusted my defeated posture. I assessed the jail facility and connected it to the decisions I have a big hand in as a county official.

Once I switched from pointing fingers at others to accepting the four fingers pointed back at me, I exhaled a sigh of relief. I have never gravitated to playing blame games or throwing pity parties. Contrarily, I understood I could have employed a better course of action. Before sunset, I forgave myself and readied my petition for forgiveness from others, especially my in-home love tank, my loving wife. The legacy I built flashed before my eyes like a lightning bolt. God had my heightened attention.

After an embarrassing four hours, the police released me into the hands of my good friend Winston. He was my voice of reason on numerous occasions. In the last eighteen years of our friendship, we formed an unbreakable bond. On that note, there was also a nonverbal contract that we would be each other's brotherly keepers.

Come hell or high waters, I could always count on Winston. Originally from South Carolina, Winston built a sizable law firm. Although we both came from similar backgrounds, we refused to succumb to glass ceilings. While neither of us carried the badge of rags to riches, we made some championing strides from public housing to leading homeowners.

After we entered his car, I mentally prepared myself for his unsolicited legal counsel, knowing that his suggestions would be exactly what I needed to hear, whether I liked it or not. There was no one else to blame, no one to point the finger at; it was all on me. I had to take full responsibility for my choices that got me into that devastating pit. Winston checked me over to ensure I was mentally and physically intact. Then he immediately delivered the needed tough love. Through the lens of a licensed attorney, Winston verbalized the dangers associated with my actions. Once I sat in the passenger seat and strapped on my seat belt, I attentively listened to his words.

"Dude, you can't do that. You have come too far," he stated as we exited the parking lot.

"You're right." I agreed, knowing in my heart of hearts he was one hundred percent correct.

Next, he strongly conveyed more legal advice and high hopes for my future. Despite this minor setback, Winston never swayed regarding his belief in me and my trajectory. What a friend in need! His presence embodied my greatest mentors both on Earth and in Heaven.

After rattling off the negative ramifications of this public display of non-Oz behavior, he read my body language and could tell I was burned out. He altered his tone from assertive to affirmative. Then, he proposed a solution-oriented option. "Look, dude. Do I need to take you to a hotel? Is this chaos going to restart if you go home? One wrong move and puff! You can lose everything you strived so hard to build."

I responded to his genuine query, "No, I am fine. I can go home. I need to see my wife. I need to apologize for acting like a bat out of hell."

Little did he know, I was all fought out; not even an ounce of fumes remained, even if I wanted to engage in productive communication. Amidst this struggle, I had grounded myself and moved into the right headspace. My only overarching goal was to get home, shower, and fix what I broke, hoping it was not shattered beyond repair. By the same token, I was equally grateful he offered a buffer to mayhem and stood ready to bail me out.

Just like that, in a mismanaged millisecond, everything changed. All I had to do was get a glimpse of where I came from. Such reflection automatically reminded me why I could not afford to start all over again. I had come too far to sink this ship because of unmerited feelings and excessive sensitivity. Temporarily, I ignored my mortal limitations, that I was also a human being with emotional intelligence. My time management, workload, relationship, and overall character were forced to adjust. Otherwise, I could ready myself to wave the white flag and give up, watching my crafted life go down the drain. Absolutely not! I quickly accepted accountability for my actions, vowing to overcome this incalculable occurrence.

Like clockwork, the regularly scheduled Tuesday meeting for our Board of Commissioners occurred the next day. I re-engaged my morning routine, including a power walk and prayer, then prepared myself for work. It was time to face the heat and address the incident head-on. At the top of the meeting, I humbly read my statement and waited for my colleagues to pose any lingering, burning questions. No one requested an explicit explanation of the previous night's event or an impromptu resignation. Maybe they, too, were aware that each person is a walking testament of grace with a few skeletons in the closet. Ironically, they, too, had found peace with my human error. We moved on with the subsequent items on the agenda. What a relief! By operating in a spirit of full transparency, I garnered their heightened respect and simultaneously catapulted myself to a greater level of authentic service. I have never publicly revisited this incident until now. Being honest and transparent will always pay dividends, even if living as an open book is difficult.

Now, it is perfect timing for global readers to see world leaders as the flawed, worthy human beings we are. Extend to us some grace as we take full responsibility for our actions. Leadership is ownership! Blaming others closes your eyes to the lesson behind the chaotic, mind-boggling event. Naturally, it may be easier to blame others until you steal away to a quiet place to genuinely reflect on the chain of events. Supporters are more likely to forgive leaders who hold themselves accountable for their behavior and address it on a public platform. This act is a proverbial practice of regaining trust and inadvertently asking for forgiveness. After all, God calls us to forgive others as he has forgiven us. I briefly allowed my suppressed feelings to take me out of my character, hence the foolish explosion. Yet this shameful inconvenience served as an urgent wake-up call from God. And boy, does he know how to interrupt your rise and regain your full attention.

Sustainable leadership, health, and success emerge when people establish consistent boundaries. From experience, I have learned the dangers of being available and active 100% of the time, answering calls or working towards a goal every waking hour. All parties suffer. While it may be easily overlooked, given my constant presence in the community, I, too, am a devoted husband, father, and church member. I created this chaotic life. All things are possible through Christ, who strengthened me then and He continues to do so now.

Unfabricated Character And Reflections

Although men dutifully attempt to mask their emotions and carry the world on their shoulders like a modern-day Iron Man, the real world proves that this emotional suppression is not sustainable or healthy in any way for anyone. Following this decision to be less vocal and transparent about the inner workings of their psychological state, exponential dangers emerge. Men generally seek out unhealthy resolutions that can contribute to a shocking downfall, sometimes irreversibly. As a male's mental capacity spirals downward, former vices may resurface. These distractions may come in destructive, sometimes irreversible forms of alcohol, drugs, adultery, pornography, gambling, and, worst of all, suicide.

Forbes magazine cited a recent survey by Slack, a messaging application and collaborative platform leveraged by organizations. It found that burnout is rising globally, but most significantly in the United States. Here, 43% of middle managers reported burnout, more than any other worker group. The statistics alone, in addition to personal conflicts, should serve as a big eye-opener to the state of exhaustion prevalent in this country. Failure to correctly identify a brewing breakdown increases the chances of a debilitating setback. These results are downright alarming and scary, although if we stop and think about the typical American life, we should not be surprised. I needed this minor infraction, as it serves a consistent reminder to nurture my emotional well-being as a norm.

There is a big price to pay when one signs up to be iconic. When you are in the limelight, leading a county or guiding a people along a large platform, attacks are consistently in the making, but so is our omnipotent Creator. This is vital to remember. Every day I want to please God, make my family proud, do good in my community, serve the greater good, and give back; however, it is tough. Living consistently under a scrutinizing spotlight infringes upon your personal space and comes with the job. Always held in high esteem, there is hardly ever an opportunity to let one's hair down or just utter a quick curse word! Damn! Give me a break before I break.

Being Oz Nesbitt, Sr. ain't easy, but I take considerable pride in being me. I, too, am a work in progress; just as fine art starts as an elementary concept and then manifests into an art piece. I am the appreciating asset in my life's story. I have screwed up more times than I care to shake a stick at, but I accept my imperfect makeup. A character-building test often accompanies the daily decision to answer my life's calling. I can only evolve into a better believer and community leader by leaning into these tests, whether in the public eye or private space. Even with God's full armor, I am not an indestructible human but a flawed person with feelings, unequivocally committed to a promising future.

Such a bright destiny does not come without an antagonistic plot by evil forces. This is nothing new on Earth. Our Creator foresees the pain on the other side of bad choices. Fortunately, he still devises a tactical plan for you to rise from the ashes. We are all engaged in a spiritual battle. In the Bible, the enemy came only to steal, kill, and destroy. It studies, watches, and waits until your most vulnerable moment to strike. The spirit of the enemy will infect those closest to you, such as your family, allies, and colleagues. Then, when you least expect it, it pops up and shows its ugly head. Yes, friends, it is that devious wolf in sheep's clothing. The strike can be quite deadly and disastrous.

Yet we must dig deep and keep going, even when our eyes carry puddles of tears. Such a burden seems too heavy to carry on our backs alone. That is when we call on Jesus, who reminds us that his burden is easy and his yoke is light. Do not give the enemy too much credit. Sure, I know that the devil is a clever, wicked spirit who strikes at the most opportune moments, shattering your world like a grenade. Ironically, in both instances I unexpectedly found myself behind bars, short-lived as they were, it was on account of small technicalities. More importantly, these unfavorable attacks were directly attached to multiple people carrying a big piece of my heart, my wife and children. Hence, it was a double-whammy-skewed attempt to dismantle my legacy. Like Paul and Jesus' other disciples in the Bible, it pained me but also promoted me to the next level as a better version of myself.

Unforeseen battles have a unique way of chiseling us into a more profound rendering of ourselves. If I reviewed the male protagonists who stretched their faith and fortified their character, I would resemble Paul. He often wrestled with a dichotomy of two opposites: his past self and future being. Depending on the season, he struggled with old desires and temptations. Sometimes Paul turned back into Saul and re-engaged in his less polished and childish ways. Yet, through God's amazing saving grace, he entered introspective therapy. Paul's captivity letters reflected his internal struggle to cast out immature, self-defeating habits. There is a common thread of rejoicing amid burdensome trials, shackled by conflict and confusion. Such liberating tasks encourage a person to practice the art of forgiveness and persistence. God will disrupt our flow to re-engage our spirit and refuel our faith. He certainly did with mine. I celebrate this blemished memory as a constant reminder to recommit to my ever-growing maturity, wisdom, and legacy.

On a large scale, capitalism places immense stress on breadwinners and leaders. Such societal constructs trickle down to the household, where families raise children to be independent thinkers and emotionally durable. This rearing style reduces their ability to be effective communicators and planners. Personally, I combat this plausible outcome by making self-reflection an immovable habit in my daily routine. I frequently escape to my nature cave and find refuge. Since I am always on for my community and family, only in this haven can I hear God's still, small voice. Outside, within my screened porch, it is just me and the birds. No one asking questions, no one casting judgments. Occasionally, I light a cigar and play Al Green on my Bluetooth speaker to reach a meditative state that calms my soul. Ah, I have found this routine practice of indulging in this nirvana immensely rewarding.

Contrary to popular belief, the number of people rooting for your winning streak far outweighs the unqualified group who do not. The latter is simply a handful of misguided people sitting on the edge of their seats looking for a good gossip line to initiate. They are hopeless creators praying that you fumble, drop your blessing, and throw away your hard-earned good life. Believe it or not, these antagonistic beings have no hope of stealing your spot. These imposters would run faster than Usain Bolt if the positions you held fell into their lap. Simultaneously, since they are fully aware that they cannot and do not want to be you, they simply cannot stand the evident favor in your life. Nevertheless, their failure to positively maximize their days on Earth is not a cemented stop sign for your meaningful journey.

While it is human nature to initially focus on the negative, especially during times of trial, try to keep your eyes on the prize. Do not become preoccupied with the bad and ignore the good, especially when only one percent may be bad. The remaining majority is upright. If you are in a compromising situation or under immense pressure, take a moment to reassess your priorities. Reset and restart the race. Keep trudging along and win big!

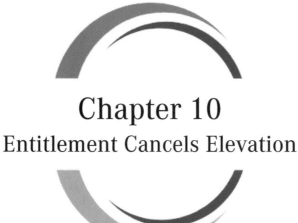

Chapter 10
Entitlement Cancels Elevation

As millions of hopeful people, inclusive of children, fled violent uprisings in Syria and Myanmar, another natural disaster flipped the worlds of Indonesia upside down in 2018. After an earthquake struck Indonesia in September, a deadly tsunami and landslides wiped out astonishing and devastating numbers of established homes, businesses, and lives. The death toll reached two thousand people as the world united to help this country rebuild. Distraught and discouraged, Indonesians, like Syrians, were forced to pick up the pieces and start anew, rebuilding their lives from scraps.

As the number eight symbolizes new beginnings, the prior number seven is equated to closure. Citizens from all social classes dropped the bug of Chairman in my ear during a few interactions. Yet my spirit told me to be still. I obliged. At this point in my life, I knew better than to recklessly jump at new opportunities, no matter how beneficial or timely they might seem. Experiences taught me valuable lessons in discernment and patience. Then, the call knocked on my door again. God said, "Move, Oz." The number eight, in its physical form, can represent perfect timing. Just as quickly as sand rushes from one end of the time capsule to the other, the minute to jump into a unique dimension with new expectations arrives. Now it was time to turn the page to draft a new beginning for Rockdale and the Nesbitt family.

To increase my readiness for a raised and more challenging level of responsibility, I treated each week as an opportunity for hands-on learning. Since winning my first election, I have immersed myself in the government world while learning the inner workings of Rockdale's unique landscape. From the county clerk to seasoned executives, I voluntarily worked under their tutelage as their tenacious apprentice. The county clerk schooled me on the county ordinances, the framework for effective meetings, rules, and regulations. Then, she switched to her other role as the executive director of government affairs. My unofficial, firsthand education transpired under the tutelage of this multifaceted professional. Given her dual function, she taught me the intricacies of public policy, legislative activities, and coordinating efforts with key stakeholders. As their unofficial pupil, I soaked up every ounce of knowledge like a sponge, hungry for their expertise. Such an intimate training ground allowed me to garner the tactics and lessons to run the county.

After eight years as the county commissioner, the perfect time for me to switch gears had arrived. It was time for me to serve my community in a greater capacity. The prospects were thrilling beyond measure, but I took my preparation for my potential new position in serious stride. Running for Chairman, I had to be 100% vested in the campaign. It was all or nothing. I sacrificed my part-time elected position to honor the eligibility guidelines, meaning no additional income. This sobering, somewhat scary decision emphatically proved my sheer dedication to the job. So, I jumped and never lost sight of who the omnipotent Provider was. Once my hat was in the bag, my Super Bowl campaign commenced.

During this season, I never ran against the opposition but towards the field goal, the desired office at hand. While I could have focused my energies on tackling my opponents, which were Oden, Hadley, and Dillard at that time, I did not. I invested my laser-focused energy in winning the hearts of the voters again. Too many candidates fixate too much on annihilating their opponents and persuading voters never to elect them rather than on the virtues of why they should vote for themselves. I chose to rise above such common temptations to win by these disingenuous means.

Campaigning evolved to be second nature for my team and me. Yet we still hit the ground running like it was our first time. Since we built a household brand, our strategy this time was to tap into those established relationships and business partnerships. By being a high school coach, a sales manager, an elected official, and an overall good neighbor, my name, Oz, was well known throughout the county. Naturally, I delivered a first-hand experience of who I was for twenty years, soon being coined the "go-to guy." This title of dependability reflected my visible commitment to our voters. At any point a taxpayer needed quick action, the listening citizen offered an assured solution: "Call Oz; he will get it done." I built this name recognition from the ground up by gaining hands-on training in my county position. Building this trustworthy reputation commanded my sweat and time for nearly a decade, but seeing citizens get prompt solutions made every day I served worthwhile. Such results were due to my character, knowledge, and experience.

Regarding another election season, it was all for Oz game time. I skillfully leveraged my tenure in government by posing this question to voters: "If I worked for you as Commissioner and achieved these results, imagine what we can accomplish together with me as your CEO and Chairman?" Nothing speaks better than the consistent actions of a leading player. Given my long track record of being an action-taker and tangible Commissioner, this query created strong buy-in from those who benefited from county-wide improvements. Think about it; when you are sailing on a cruise to the crystal-blue water of a Caribbean destination, you want to arrive safe and sound. That withstanding, do you want the lead captain to be someone who graduated from Mariner's school last week or a graduate with five-plus years under their belt? For the passenger who does not want to be stuck in the ocean, choosing an experienced professional backed by a cohesive crew is a no-brainer.

As I assessed this race, the polls conveyed I was the unstated underdog to the opposing candidate. The incumbent was a familiar history maker I knew quite well, Mr. Richard Oden, the two-term, first Black Chairman of Rockdale County. Even with the county's mixed sentiments around his confident approach to claiming his throne, he won the elections fair and square. Coined as King Richard in multiple publications, Oden took considerable pride in being a trailblazer, accruing dozens of personal accolades. On a professional scale, as expected, Oden's subordinates wanted more. In listening to the leadership in the corporate office, employees openly discussed their discontentment with the county plateau. I grew frustrated with the slow progression, too, then decided I could keep watching from the sidelines or get in the game. It became obvious that his season was nearing the final days of his eighth year.

Campaigning allowed ample opportunities for candidates to highlight their strengths and clarify their intentions. While Oden leveraged his past wins, I drove home my time-proven, tried-and-true, people-driven approach. And, in 2016, Rockdale County voted to elect us as Chairman. Although the voting ballots only listed my government name, my newly elected role embodied a package deal, including my supportive family and friends. I knew their unwavering investments and consistent prayers catapulted me to another level. To think I climbed the political ladder on my merit would be futile and ego-driven. Any acquaintance or voter who met me also concurred that my Aunt Mattie and Momma did not raise such a pompous fool but rather a humble leader. I owed my success to their good grooming and to the will of a loving God who led me to use my spiritual gifts for the betterment of my community. I have always tried to live my life according to the two greatest commandments: to love God and to love my neighbor as myself. Hence, I honored Oden in his final days of office and assured him I would continue the magnificent work he initiated.

Once sworn into my new role in 2017, I began constructing a sustainable, core leadership conglomerate. First, I created a community improvement team to enhance the day-to-day experiences for all families. Secondly, I committed to empowering the executive staff by investing in their national training. These individuals collaborated with like-minded leaders from other counties and returned with sharpened skill sets. As an experienced government official, I learned early on that the leading protagonist must form a dynamic team to champion a greater cause beyond one's immediate household.

Upon transitioning to politics, one of my primary objectives was to operate as a way-maker. My top objective was to serve as a bridge from my current position to a sea of opportunities, much like senators, lawyers, citizens, and family had done for me. I also brought selected qualified allies with me. These ambitious professionals demonstrated their ability to support my established objectives via their consistent and impactful roles along my former campaign trails. Of this hand-selected group, the majority exhibited the loyalty, integrity, and work ethic our office needed.

Additionally, I sourced two of the brightest and most ambitious men of Rockdale County to serve as my righthand men. Modern rockstars and burgeoning leaders in their own right, I witnessed these two move rooms with their words and impact the community in multiple arenas for nearly fifteen years. Collectively, we would infuse Rockdale with a Buckhead experience wrapped in golden traditions. I offered them a six-figure salary, benefits, and the opportunity to get their feet wet in government. What more could one ask for? But these quick promotions morphed into a chaotic monsoon of frivolous acts. Another test of my agility and perseverance was about to rock my world.

In 2018, discord erupted when I least expected it. Then, between 2019 and 2020, the harmonious rockstar team I built erupted into clashing waves of division. Many robust personalities and personal ambitions induced an in-house trifecta that shook my key team to its core. Like the unexpected tsunami in Indonesia, our organization's infrastructure was dismantled seemingly overnight. I truly could not have seen this devastation due to egos coming. Before I could project the need to post job openings or even receive resignation letters, my team crumbled. The key decision-makers collaborating with me around the boardroom table began an unforeseeable purge. These eliminations were not a result of budget cuts or retirement but a non-cohesive vision. The discord excavated grueling holes in our ship as we rowed ahead, barely keeping our heads above the crashing waves.

Unfortunately, after less than two years as Chairman, my two proteges proved to be controversial employees who shook our established infrastructure and our mentor-mentee relationship's once-strong foundation. As disruptive clashes between vetted leaders with contrasting visions emerged, so did deeply seated convictions regarding personal goals and unilateral moves. These two increased their standard of living and entertained lavish outings. Such expedient lifestyle changes caused a sense of urgency for promotions and additional pay. Climbing the ladder became an overnight sensation desiring immediate results or job abandonment. Each unrealistic ultimatum communicated via divisive actions left me hurt and blindsided.

Ironically, I stood as a strong proponent of professional growth and career progression, but not overnight. There was and still is not a magical elevator to take a person from an entry-level position to an executive position at the snap of a finger, as much as overly ambitious folks might wish otherwise. Just as I had invested decades in learning the ins and outs of government as a police officer and a Commissioner, I naturally expected my two mentees to do the same by respecting and honoring a similar time-invested journey. Yet this was not the case. Lateral moves were no longer appealing to a pair of covetous employees. Not only did they desire promotions and pay raises, but they were even gunning for my newly acquired position. It is disheartening what short-sighted greed can do to a man's heart. No one is above reproach.

On the brink of change, a person's attitude and approach can be the life or death of their career. The three ugly E's, emotions, egos, and entitlement, put the proverbial nail in the coffin quickly and unexpectedly. Unlike the previous five to ten years, separations and resignations flooded our formerly cohesive organization. Short-term thinking and minimal patience led key personnel to believe they were entitled to more pay and benefits. As research-based denials met their unmerited requests, their egos flared up. Emotions ran wild. An unchecked sense of self and unhealthy feelings disseminated catastrophic dangers throughout the workplace. These two elements can place a chokehold on one's judgment and career trajectory, to the misfortune of all involved parties.

Over the course of six months, the office transformed into a competitive landscape instead of a collaborative backdrop. While their job satisfaction was paramount in the accelerated betterment of Rockdale County, as the leading figure of our newly knitted organization, I also understood that one decision from a disgruntled teammate could knock hard-earned progress four steps backward. Lethal egos continued to rear their ugly heads alongside self-righteous entitlement. Unfortunately, the sullen few unequivocally ignored the truth that the world does not owe anyone a thing. Wins must be earned. To boldly narrate the likelihood of waking up and becoming Chairman in one year was not only presumptuous and distasteful but also far-fetched. Why would anyone in their right mind attempt to unseat the person who hired them? This would not be tolerated on my watch. Something had to be done.

Before reacting to their third rant around the office, I packed my briefcase and headed home to my peace, grateful I still had my safe place. When I stole away to my back deck to reflect on the workplace shenanigans, I strolled down Memory Lane to my youthful, overly zealous days. Thankfully, during my doses of immature, big-headed acts, community leaders or close family members quickly scolded and corrected me. Such hasty adjustments prompted a permanent memory where humility saved my life.

Later in adulthood, my mother planted herself in the Harrisburg Community, living in a quaint apartment on the western end of Broad Street. While riding my bike down the sidewalk across from Harrisburg Bait and Tackle Shop, a car filled with white people exhibiting delinquent behaviors came along. As they caught sight of me jovially riding, these misguided teens jumped the curve and hit me. I flew off my bike. Like bats out of hell, they drove off chanting racist epitaphs and celebrating as if they had luckily hit the Georgia Lottery. Once I landed on my back, I raised my head up to memorize their car plate, committed to making them pay for this crime and bankrupt their hatred. Unfortunately, it was a temporary tag issued by Jim Satcher Ford, preventing any chance of holding these knuckleheads accountable. Then, I glanced across the street and noticed an older white couple staring at me. Instead of calling the police or coming to my aid, they remained glued to the bench as if nothing happened. Their silence angered me more than the back-breaking pain circulating throughout my body. By the same token, I sighed, knowing the leadership of my elders helped me bite my tongue and stand back on my feet. Such short-lived, hurtful, and prideful moments were often dismantled before they could disrupt my ascension. Hence, I vowed to remain humble and true to my authentic self throughout my professional reign.

On paper, my two proteges offered the perfect resume inked with considerable experience and immense potential. So, I decided to initiate some tough but necessary conversations individually and collectively. My high hopes for their future were sentiments that remained constant. I reiterated the progression formula of time plus tenure. Not only did their request need board approval but they also were connected to a hierarchical time clock. Within our organization, other employees paid the cost in time and energy, elapsing the five- and ten-year marks. To grant a pay increase that superseded the more tenured workers' take-home pay would not only be wrong but destructive. Even though I presumed we were all moving forward on one accord after our meeting, I was mistaken.

Imagine the dismay when I discovered there was a Judas amongst us. My right-hand man poured out his deepest secrets in my office. I created a safe place for him to communicate any nagging drivers causing his consistent request. I even offered him budgeting tips to scale back his expenses. To no avail, in time, it was brought to my attention that my key man was punching holes in our county master plan. He was orchestrating an outright coup right beneath my nose while smiling in my face. In his attempt to seize power, he garnered the attention of my department heads and started framing me as the enemy. Although he denied such acts, I lost respect and trust for him in one swoop. *Why didn't he just ask what is the probability or possibility of me getting an increase?* I wondered to myself. Like Judas, he brazenly betrayed me and established his agenda that opposed me, the same man who held him in high regard. Every move he made was done with his spin and ulterior motives. From that point, his requests and recommendations fell upon deaf ears, as I could barely see past character flaws, I recently became purview to during his employment.

In the other corner office sat my left-hand man in charge of my public image and media relations. This unwarranted betrayal was Judas's level on steroids. Their deceptive acts pierced my side like the sharp teeth of jaws ripping away a piece of my heart. While at Rockdale High School, I met this fourteen-year-old kid I decided to mentor. I was there for every milestone he accomplished, graduating from high school, getting his degree from UGA, and even working at my former radio station, offering applause and advice. When it was time to run my campaign in 2016, he managed it excellently, which led me to hire him. On paper, his resume showed his extensive background in media and public relations. Yet, as bills came in, the financial pinch erroneously led him to jump ship with my other chief employee. Then, he haphazardly employed his acute writing skills to draft an insulting letter to me. Of course, I checked him on those unprofessional acts. Although I did not fire him, I gave him a stern response like the verbal lashing a father would deliver to a son. Instead of learning from this mistake, he abandoned his post later that week.

For the two proteges who left my mind perplexed, they crushed a piece of my heart. To their demise, self-centered ambition muted their voice of reasoning. Any remaining hope that these executives would come around sooner rather than later vanished. Perhaps these guys would revisit their timetable and come to grips with the years of experience needed to secure a promotion. Unfortunately, they did not. Regrettably, they did not. To date, neither one has yet to own their missteps outrightly. When I encounter them in public places, I extend immense respect and sincere concern for their future successes. In fact, when people call to inquire about these two guys, I give them five stars on their ability to execute their job obligations. I do not hold grudges. Although they did not completely burn the bridge, they created a bouldering barrier. It has a flag stuck on it to remind me of their potential to sink a sailing ship.

Outside of those two, I sourced from Rockdale; our CFO was a trusted ally to whom I credit much of my success and the county's financial wellness. This qualified woman possessed the institutional knowledge of the county, in addition to financial acumen that would wow any big-time investor. This adept woman built a financial footing for twenty years, spurring Rockdale's sustainability. When I started as the new CEO, she willfully showed me the ropes. I was beyond grateful. Her job separation was a great loss. Her shoes have not been filled yet. Temporary hires start and quickly fire themselves when given the tall task of managing the monetary landscape of an entire county. I always played out distinct courses of action for these corporate restructuring bouts but left it in God's hands.

Inevitably, this season of new beginnings kicked off with losses. Not only did I second-guess my mentorships, but I also questioned the character of those I had invested in for years. There was no more trust and loyalty. I held out hope that the relationships were salvageable, that my two MVPs would wake up from their deep sleep in the depths of pride. These two reminded me of promising high school students who go from minimum-wage fast-food jobs to the NFL. Such a fast promotion from a humble lifestyle to a strikingly upscale one places the newcomer in a fragile place. Depending on their inner circle, the player either earns and doubles the millions or exhausts every financial resource trying to keep up with the Joneses. Only with wisdom and experience, egotistical or misguided adults can come to their senses. At that point, their delivery proves God's grace is still sufficient, and growth is still a winning antidote.

Earn Your Space In The Workplace

A wise man once said, "Be careful who you let on your ship because some people will sink the whole ship just because they can't be the captain." When identifying your key circle, pay close attention to the person behind the tailored suit and charisma. Sometimes, the person underneath the prestigious attire is narcissistic, waiting to take your position. This takeover is not because the person has a more grandiose vision or work ethic than you. On the contrary, this individual craves the power seat because it feeds their ego. The world is a dog-eat-dog arena, with wolves in sheep's clothing around every corner. Proceed with utmost caution.

During a storm, the safest action is to be steady and still. Anyone who chooses to panic during a dangerous or tumultuous situation increases the likelihood of demise. For example, a lifeguard calmly assesses a swimmer in danger before acting. Then, this rescuer only approaches a drowning person when the person stops fighting the water. Fighting the strong tide and flailing arms while ensuring the guard's safety is impossible. Otherwise, the intense panic could result in injuries, even fatalities. The enemy attacks when you are exhausted or, dare I say, when you are highest on your pedestal. Be sure to check your ego at the door, friend. Pride is vanity, a sin that is truly deceiving. It blindsides us. Often, we need to fall before we realize what has happened. You find the Rock and your authentic self at rock bottom. Remain steady in the storm. Draw close to the purpose that your divine Creator has instilled in you. Keep your eyes and heart on Him.

Building a company culture with visionaries subscribed to a unified vision is a miracle. One trusted ally of this reliable circle will be deemed the righthand man. For example, there is only one Ironman to one War Machine, one Moses and one Joshua, one Ralph David Abernathy to one Dr. Martin Luther King. Such a partnership insulates principal change agents from direct, unnerving attacks. Honestly, I never intended for my direct hires to be my number two or three forever. It would have been a great honor to pass them the torch after my final run. In the interim, these two would have witnessed the sacrifices, sugar water, mayonnaise sandwiches, and growth of the position of such a tall order required from the incumbent.

For those who are eyeing a government position, I propose these queries:

1. What are your motives for serving in a government position?
2. Are you willing to leave your comfort zone to make the necessary sacrifices to grow into that position?

3. How are you planning to continue the progression of the city, county, state, or country that elects you?

After winning a few elections, I know that it is vital that you are crystal clear about your intended goals. My goal was to create a place with more positive, professional, and progressive milestones. Each time I speak to the power of the three A's, attitude, approach, and appearance, I am reminded of how these elements enhanced my journey. Whenever you run your race at your own pace on your path, some people feel neglected, as you are no longer catering to their self-righteous needs. Do not be moved by their quest to knock you off your game. There are bound to be detours and potholes along any adventure. Always remember and respect the person who throws you a rescue tube, the lifeline to a winning opportunity. That person is a keeper, a true brother in arms.

"Don't settle for average.

Bring your best to the moment.

Then,

whether it fails or succeeds,

at least you know

you gave all you had."

—Angela Bassett

Chapter 11
Voyage of Being My Brother's Keeper

O n May 21, 2023, the prestigious Morehouse College fostered its 139th commencement exercise on its venerable campus. As the only male institution in the Atlanta University Center, this college carried worldwide recognition as a melting pot for aspiring, promising Black students who exuded confidence and vision. Global publications consistently rank this liberal arts school as an ivy league institution, falling in the top ten Historically Black Colleges and Universities year after year. Now, my youngest son, Evynn, was becoming a part of that history. Of course, his proud squad arrived in full village style, with three vehicles jam-packed with smiling avid supporters. We were Evynn's fans, who would clap and shriek from the stands while he crossed the stage. We entered the front gates thirty minutes early to compensate for Atlanta's notorious traffic and parking, which can be an inevitable headache for latecomers.

Passing the towering statue of Dr. Martin Luther King as we entered King's Chapel, I pondered; *these fellow brothers are making impressive historical strides, defying countless odds, and making their families proud.* Empty seats began filling up with parents, family, and friends, in high anticipation of witnessing first-hand the top echelon of ambitious and gifted young men achieve a bachelor's degree from the exclusive league of HBCUs. As we patiently awaited these tenacious, soon-to-be graduates, flashback moments permeated my excited mind in an accelerated but emotionally rushing nature to the days when I had been slated to be a bachelor's, degree-totting man.

In 1996, Voorhees College, an accredited HBCU based in Denmark, South Carolina, just across the Savannah River, constructed a satellite location in North Augusta. This grand opening also included a flexible adult education component. With that addition, working professionals could pursue a degree and maintain their livelihood simultaneously, undoubtedly a much-needed route for adults far into the middle of their careers. So, the night school option seemed appealing and feasible at the cross-section of marriage and fatherhood. I would work as a police officer, dine with my family, then immerse my final hours into my studies. I entered this new chapter with high hopes.

When I scanned the classrooms, it was obvious that this course load encompassed a duality of hard and easy for most adult learners. Hence, I voluntarily led a tutorial group for those pursuing an Organizational Management degree, as this specialty was right up my alley. A couple of hours a week, I helped my classmates grasp community engagement and human resources concepts, which came naturally to me. On the contrary, those math courses were in another lane and gave me a run for my money. Algebraic functions and statistics leaped from my secondary school days and pounced on my educational goal like a fierce tiger attacking his prey. I was the poor prey. Mathematics courses created a fury snowball effect of challenges. Standing at the bottom of a huge mountain, I distressingly watched an avalanche of low grades roll down in my direction. Once I conveyed these pesky nuances of required courses to Aunt Mattie, she immediately switched on her solution mode. Desperate to spare her nephew from failing a class, she dialed the person with the solutions in the palm of her hands, or better yet, in her brain: her goddaughter, Monique. Not only was she a true mathematician, but she was also like the younger sister I never had. When Aunt Mattie conveyed her request to tutor me, she was ecstatic. As a recent graduate of Benedict College, she understood the rigor of collegiate courses and was eager to help me cross that bridge too.

Once my account reflected the receipt of my second student loan, life as a college student was in full swing. Initially, Monique and I established a viable schedule, two evenings per week. The only payment she would accept was my giving her an invitation to my pending graduation ceremony. Her teaching skills were stellar, but life's demands were mounting feverishly. After investing two years, I hung my college student coat on the rack. Although this was an incomplete mission, I remain a strong advocate for educational advancements. In fact, not only have I increased the tuition reimbursement funding for county employees, but I also spearheaded multiple small business seminars to educate entrepreneurs. Education can serve as a great equalizer.

Fast forward, as the father to two daughters who graduated, I now had the honor of watching my son reach one of the lifetime goals Aunt Mattie had planted into my peripheral during my adolescence. This was a family celebration day like none other. There is no way she was not hitting a praise dance in Heaven. Some things proliferate across multiple generations. The stillness of the chapel, as the men progressed down its two aisles against the widespread instrumental, was euphoric. While hundreds of young men carried honors cords, the visible camaraderie and unmasked excitement captured me. This exuberance would not release me. These brave souls had to pivot and charge forward amid the global pandemic insighted by COVID-19. Unfortunately, every living person did not make it to the next month, the next year, or the next graduation season. Watching hundreds march synchronized and coordinated in their freshly polished black shoes and white-collar shirts below their gowns encouraged me to reconsider completing my bachelor's degree anew.

Before four hundred seniors heard their names called and rightfully turned their tassels, keynote speaker Wes Moore, Maryland's first Black governor and the third in the United States, took the stage. A proud husband and sibling of three, he craftily channeled his authorship and leadership into infusing a great charge into the virtuous souls of the graduating body. After receiving an honorary doctorate from Morehouse, and extended credit to his godfather, a Morehouse alumnus, Dr. Trailor, class of 1953, his speech commenced. Wes Moore meticulously turned back the pages to the historical figures, their fights, prayers, sacrifices, and victories that made college degrees attainable for generations to come. From Union soldiers who diligently fought for freedom to the assiduously civil rights leaders who battled for non-biased equity, such women and men paved the way. Then, the dean read the graduates' names, and these joy-filled victors joined the ranks of legendary Morehouse Men, like Senator Raphael Warnock, Mayor Randall Woodfin of Alabama, Pastor Jamal Bryant, and former American Express CEO Kenneth Chenault. History and the present day were now being infused with another round of trailblazers seated in their caps and gowns.

After being officially inducted into the Morehouse alumni via their degree attainment, we happily gathered outdoors under the beaming afternoon sun. Once Evynn joined us, each of us extended words of encouragement and congratulatory hugs. This was the second occasion when all three women I married at some point were in the same space and for an epic event, nonetheless. Then, I thought, *Oh my, I played an intricate role in this legendary outcome.* I was literally witnessing a historical moment that registered with me like the best Black Lifetime movie yet but without the catty drama and melancholy. I could do without those.

Whoever said blended families could not create a healthy, prosperous, and successful village was unequivocally wrong. Before my very eyes, my eldest son and his wife were expecting their first child. My former wives, college graduates, and educational advocates had also fostered a sisterhood beyond my wildest imagination. Everyone was genuinely happy to celebrate legacy wins and growth. What a high! What a blessing from God!

I admirably nodded my head in observation of my sons' brotherly interaction. Oz Jr. placed his hand on Evynn's shoulder, and everyone present could see the admiration in his eyes for his baby brother. Such imagery incited my reflection on those joyous moments within my brotherhood mosaic and was flooded with some groundbreaking experiences we shared.

At that point, my baby brother, Zachary, resided on the West Coast in Texas. Growing up, he was our in-house comedian. Take a moment and picture the typical American stand-up comedian and reputable actor, Kat Williams, telling jokes as a middle school student in the center of the living room. Laughter prompted by him could be felt in the deepest cradle of your stomach. It brought tears to your eyes. Outside of his random class clown moments, Zachary was a people person and a keen mathematician. If you asked him to calculate the amount of money it would take for every person in the world to have potable, lead-free water from Flint, Michigan, to Eritrea, he could probably compute it in his head. He embodied the computational skills for the two of us, plus a few more.

Once he graduated and matriculated to Benedict College, his reputation magnified and followed him those seventy-three miles from Augusta to campus. Not too long after successfully completing his freshman year, Zachary became known as the life of the party. Ironically, two or three semesters later, I joined him in Columbia, South Carolina, when I accepted a nine-month contract. One unfortunate night, the dispatcher paged the police, requiring assistance shutting down a disturbing party. I intercepted the call readying myself to de-escalate the situation. *What college does not have parties that make the roof pop off and the walls shake?* I wondered. This was nothing new under the sun. However, another patrol officer who was closer to the commotion went. The radio chatter silenced. I presumed the event ended, and every attendee made it out alive and peacefully returned to their dorms.

On my way home, I stopped by the station. Upon entry, the officer asked, "Nesbitt, do you have a brother named Zachary?"

Taken aback by such a random inquiry, I paused and stared at the man straight in the eyes to ensure he was not pulling my leg. "Yes."

Then, he looked at me with a shocked expression and said, "I asked because you two carry the same last name. He may be back there in a holding cell."

Nerves afire and anxiety churning in my stomach, I curiously paced back to the holding cells, and to my daunting surprise, there he was. Zachary was hung over, cursing like an enraged sailor without an operational compass.

A hundred questions darted through my mind at that awestricken moment. Most importantly, however, he was my little brother. I knew what I had to do. I willfully bailed him out the next day when my shift ended. Together, we attended court to face his trivial charges.

After two years elapsed, managing collegiate expectations and his partying behavior proved to be an unconquerable mix, so he dropped out. Then, he morphed into a wanderer, hopping around from city to city, state to state, searching for a place to call home that spoke and reignited his God-given potential. Multiple times, my eldest brother, Gregory, and I devised a plan to rid Zachary of his inner plight and addiction to alcohol. Sadly, each plan proved to be another failed attempt at reeling my baby brother back in from the dogged streets. After a while, we made the hard decision to let Zachary live life on his terms, enduring the accompanying consequences of his choices. Still, my brother's welfare carved out a perpetual fixation in my mental space.

On the other hand, the eldest, Gregory, was quite the opposite. He relocated to Athens, GA. He established a thriving career with a local utility company and found great satisfaction in consistent ascension there. His loving wife and daughter are the twinkles of his eye. Over the years, our relationship has come full circle. As adult men, we overcame periodic contentious times sprinkled into our brotherhood after the passing of our mother. Yet, over the last twenty years, we have reclaimed and cultivated an unbreakable friendship that goes deeper than blood. It always refuels my tank to know my big brother is one of my biggest fans. In addition, he will defend me at all costs and respects me greatly. When his son unexpectedly passed away, it hit our family like a bag of bricks dropped from an Atlanta high-rise penthouse floor. Yet we held each other up, and the strength of our bond was further reinforced. After that, I conveyed an additional solution I conjured up to save our little brother.

As Thanksgiving season inched closer, Zachary and I held a few guiding conversations that led me to believe he was ready to give up the street life. Perhaps my prayers had finally been answered. Those dialogues, tangent with the hope evoked by the holiday season, provoked youthful family memories to run circles in my mind. My mother, aunt, father, and siblings ate as one united lineage during those years. Our foundation was impenetrable, but I am certain the unexpected death of my father cracked us all, yet in unique ways. To cope with losing our paternal figure, I immersed myself into the workforce, like my older brother, but Zachary submerged himself in the party world. They were undoubtedly key markers in each one of our lives. We just internalized the loss differently.

That November, I utilized a week of my vacation time to throw Zachary a lifeline. I purchased a ticket and boarded a Delta flight with managed expectations but faith-laced hopes. Then, I strategically prepared for this cross-country trip like another Super Bowl, but with a personal undertone. I read articles and consulted therapists. Research-based studies and trusted advisors forewarned me of the substantial challenges I might face.

According to the 2021 National Survey on Drug Use and Health, 28.6 million adults ages eighteen and older had Alcohol Use Disorder, which does not account for the mounting underage drinking cases. Alcoholism is a strong, unwavering addiction; some doctors have traced it to hereditary connections. Much like my father, Zachary employed drinking to wash away the day's worries. On the other hand, he did not master the work and party life as my father did. Zachary's thirty-plus-year addiction caused him to have a downward spiral, to almost be unrecognizable. As a man in his forties, he was not earning an income but being homeless, jumping around between states. Given the circumstances, I was still unwilling to bring in another new year without doing everything in my power to kickstart my brother's recovery. This would be the greatest win, the opportunity to reignite the rich Nesbitt tradition and the remaining living family unit around the dining room table. What was this restricting narrative keeping him chained to this tired life?

Once I landed, I searched for him high and low in Dallas, Texas. I purchased a cell phone and pinpointed a proven AUD program for him. Once I located him, wrapped in a blanket adjacent to a dark, dank bridge, we grabbed food and headed to the closest Walmart. We swiftly roamed the store, selecting the items from my mental list to help him brave the freezing weather, especially if he returned to the streets. Filling the cart with a winter coat, beanie hats, jeans, gloves, and a duffle bag, I hoped this visible act of concern would further motivate him to pivot and reclaim his life. This night I checked us into a hotel. My brother would rest in a decent bed like the free-spirited man he was.

After a hot breakfast, I proposed my game plan the following day, but he immediately rejected it. His pushback crushed me to my core. It hurt like burning hell. It was like that bag of bricks crushing me all over again. I should not have been surprised, as history has a way of confirming one's trajectory in the future, more often than not. Here he was, my version of a real-life Albert Einstein, but a good-looking man, consumed by perilous liquor. It was destroying him. Countless years of non-doctor monitoring epilepsy and diabetes, topped off with alcoholism, were eating him alive like grimy maggots.

Within seventy-two hours, Zachary's body shut down. Unbeknownst to me, he employed his own alcohol recovery program and detoxed cold turkey without professional monitoring. He fell to the floor, and the disastrous thump sent a death-gripping sensation throughout my soul. Of course, I witnessed such bodily convulsions as a police officer, but this health alarm had never hit so close to home until now. Fumes of alcohol poured from his skin pores. He reeked like an aged barrel of Tennessee whiskey. Once he awoke from his seizure, we immediately caught an Uber to the nearest emergency room. After running medical tests, the doctors instantly admitted him into the ICU. Taking medications and drinking alcohol was a dangerous gamble that took a toll on his withering body.

Following Zachary's discharge procedure, we navigated to the resource center I had pinpointed before my trip. The well-trained team commenced its routine eligibility procedures. Then, the counselor reviewed the onboarding process, and I could see the repulsed shift in Zachary's body language. But the standard house rules, no television, no contact with outside people, and daily curfews broke the camel's back. Before I could get a pen in Zachary's hand to facilitate his agreeing signature on these immutable guidelines, he catapulted from the seat. Instead of understanding the benefits of these restrictions, he responded, "No, I am not going to do that. I am a grown man." Then, he frantically walked out the door. My heart dropped to my stomach; it probably skipped a beat. Such an unbearable outcome forced me to readjust my hopeful expectations once again.

Needless to say, after entering his world and witnessing his condition, it seemed like he might have had nine lives. It painfully dawned on me that his obstinate decision was not changing, so I was delighted to cultivate more fond memories with him. God knows I gave saving Zachary my best shot. Begging him to reconsider was like beating a dead horse. Since he sold the cell phone I provided, I do not know if he is dead or alive at the time of this writing. Unfortunately, my entire adult life, I existed on a slight edge, expecting that disruptive, heartbreaking phone call that he was no longer with us. All that aside, he crosses my mind every single day.

The longstanding adage, "You can't teach an old horse new tricks," is clearly illustrated in rituals and routines. Whether it is your brother, spouse, or friend, the person who carries this relational tie in who they are. You cannot make people change their established opinion and behavior patterns, no matter how much you love them or wish otherwise. We are all creatures of habits. While life gurus tout it only takes twenty-one days to create a new habit, kicking a long-term addiction requires triple that amount of time and a dedicated support group. Whether a person's vice or addiction is social media, drugs, alcohol, or sweets, something hooks us. It will take the force of nature to unhook us.

Moreover, the discontinuance must be a personal decision. Then the recovery can commence. Such a pivotal shift is like teaching two guys raised in the Old South to see past color and craft an impenetrable brotherhood. Even when a person is weaned from an addiction, the resulting breakthrough is not a stamp of forever healing. Life has a way of luring us back into destructive behaviors. Just as in the Old South, remnants of racism still rear themselves today. So, this confirms how difficult change truly is.

Nearly twenty years ago, a multilayered duality of friends and strangers birthed a new brotherhood. Marty Jones, a city councilman, introduced me to Jay Grover, an iconic connector. Recently, I overheard him informing an inquisitive citizen about the laws of the land, or in our case, of Rockdale County. As a former cop with the city of Conyers, Jay was now known as the 411 informant for all places and faces residing in our zone. Over the years, he learned where all the bodies were buried and the skeletons in many closets. He added color to the idiomatic expression of shooting from the hip, as he did not hold back or water down information. Without any discriminatory lens, he called a spade a spade from a genuine place.

For the next few decades, we built a transformative bond. It was no hidden secret that we were like modern-day Frick and Frack. One glimpse at our social media images with our chipper 1 faces side by side proved that our community outings were plentiful, highlighting our newly fermented brotherhood. In fact, for one ten-year span, we routinely journeyed eastbound on I-20 to Augusta, Georgia, on Tuesdays. Here, we basked in the annual Masters tournament like modern-day kings. Premium access to five-star meals, inclusive of lobster, caviar, and steak, was served to us on a platter. In this VIP section with a balcony view to the golf tournament, secured by my Augusta connections, we mixed and mingled with the who's who of America. Between lunch and dinner, we strolled over to the pro shop and purchased paraphernalia. Such red-carpet treatment perplexed onlookers, but remember relationships can take you places money cannot.

Our years in law enforcement, coupled with our community engagement, bridged us together across color lines. We both understood the racial duality we represented as a Black and Caucasian man, but we never allowed these genetic differences to wedge a divisive space between us. At the DNA level, many differences in race are apparent but also miniscule. Sure, we disagreed on certain issues, but we always kept it real with each other. No two people, no matter how close, will ever see eye to eye on everything. Heck, even I have changed my mind on certain topics throughout my lifetime. Occasionally, we would tag team on an issue, playing good cop and bad cop, then arrive at a happy medium. For example, Jay hosted quarterly Chop It Up sessions in his abode. Against the backdrop of unifying messaging and reducing counterproductive division, these invite-only events were groundbreaking solvents. From heavyweight political officials to aspiring civic leaders, select leaders gathered to hash out disagreeing viewpoints. Intermittently, heated debates arose. It was a Black man against the Ku Klux Klan organization. Of course, no one daringly showed up dressed in dingy white sheets, as Jay had zero tolerance for that foolishness. However, such contrasting opinions rooted in ancient racism were inevitable. Skillfully, Jay undertook the role of devil's advocate, challenging all parties to reconsider their approach. By night's end, all attendees were well-fed and struck some common ground.

Selfless acts and wise counsel were two factors that strengthened our brotherhood. Jay and I were tight as thieves. Since Conyers was a fairly new landscape for me, but Jay's native land, he granted me privy to unspoken customs, bylaws, and hidden secrets. It was as if he had memorized Rockdale County's black book like the back of his hand. When a particular topic piqued my interest, or I perceived that he was brushing over the juicy details, I inquired further. What curious mind would not want the full scope? Some probes were met with direct eye contact, followed by, "Trust me, brother, you do not want to know." With a sigh of momentary disappointment, I trusted his discerning spirit. Lord knows my soul was already burdened with personal baggage. In other scenarios, after a shot or two of Crown Royal, he would divulge covert information and then swear me to secrecy.

Known as the unofficial president of the county, Jay was a genius with a political IQ off the charts. With a how-to guide on government leadership and deeply planted roots in Conyers, I often wondered why he did not run for political office. He made it noticeably clear that goal was not on his bucket list. Often, he conveyed, "I'm not a king, don't wanna be a king. I am a kingmaker!" Jay preferred to mitigate cultural divides and work from behind the scenes. I could appreciate that. We all have distinct roles to play and opposing lanes to maintain.

Then, in July 2022, another unforeseen death knocked the wind out of my lungs. Jay had passed. Not only was he my dear brother, but he was one of my closest friends. Life moves faster than a California forest fire as a person quickly seems to jump from twenty-one to sixty-five. Then too fast and too soon, planned events and control are lost. A torrent of tears profusely poured down like water bombing on burning forestry. I had no choice but to pull that proverbial car over and weep until the fuming rage ceased. A guy who just about everyone loved, the community peacemaker and go-to guy, was gone.

When I spoke at his funeral, beyond devastated, I choked on my tears. Sometimes, language fails to convey the profound depth of loss we endure when someone we cherish dies. His death was a surreal wake-up call that no living being can pinpoint the time or the hour he or she will be called home. I still have his Celebration of Life program strategically placed on my office desk. Occasionally, I will vocalize my thoughts as if he can still operate as my wise sounding board. I sometimes cry, laugh, or get a little pissed that he is no longer here in the flesh during urgent moments. Hell, I gotta load of local bull to discuss. Without a doubt, I am certain he would advise the best course of action to turn some messes into miracles. Plus, who will attend the golf tournaments with me now? Loss impacts us all in a myriad of ways. Sit with the sorrow and cope as needed. There is no concrete timetable for grief.

Be Your Brother's Flame Keeper

Every path, both started and unfinished, may be predestined by God. These walks will be accompanied by situations that cause growth and pain. The remaining scars will not fade away, so it is wise to find help. Outside of seeking refugee with God and your home-based reflection oasis, I strongly advocate for routine counseling. Therapy is a necessary self-care practice, just as completing daily exercise or your annual medical exams is. Such a commitment is not only for trauma survivors, but also those individuals dedicated to positively growing their emotional well-being and mental fortitude.

Statistics show that only in the last forty years have African American and other people of color begun to embrace treatment for mental illness and emotionally unbalanced behaviors. Although this increase in therapy is a revolutionary practice, the damage inflicted upon families previously leaves some wellness recovery scenarios unsalvageable. Before this popularity, standard, self-harming go-to's such as drug and alcohol abuse were antidotes for trouble. Unfortunately, overindulgence in these substances shortens one's life span. While intoxication provides a temporary escape from gnawing agony, the usage of such products carries damaging effects on a person's welfare. A safer, less destructive resort is available in the friendships we cultivate.

Whether the brotherhood is born out of a fraternity like the founders of Ruby Tuesday, who studied at the University of Tennessee, or the siblings you gain by paternity, such close-knit bonds lend themselves to the power of coming together to support one another. Of this inner circle, identify that loyal friend who forces you to face your challenges while simultaneously applauding your victories. Like a durable power of attorney, this entrusted individual is the gatekeeper to your reputation and the constructive criticizer. Blatantly stated, this person tells you what you need to hear at various times instead of what you want. For the same reason, this ally will rescue first and raise hell later, as would you. This platonic closeness builds a beneficial level of reciprocity and interconnectivity on autopilot. This faithful friend is steadfast, loyal, and true. Their love may be of the tough variety. Their words may hurt because sometimes the truth hurts, but it also sets us free. This person may very well be God's hands using the garden shears to prune away the dying parts of your vine so you can grow in your faith and walk with the Lord.

Epilogue
A Legacy of Passion and Persistence

The decade of 2020 interrupted our business and life-as-usual momentum. Of course, this was a forced reality for all. From the onset, these ten years served as a vivid reminder that from the moment we enter this diverse, often perplexing world, life becomes a compounding, balancing beam of decisions and dualities. At any intersection of uncomfortable growth and comfortable complacency, an array of firm decisions must be made. Whether holding firmly to a subscribed idea of success or progressing towards a collective cause, each chosen route, year after year, actively constructs our legacy. This after-life gift exceeds any monetary proceeds or lucrative assets left to loved ones. Legacy is a combination of transformative seeds planted in your community at large. Once rooted in values and vision, those faith-coated seedlings proliferate into newfound possibilities, unrestrained by inequitable weeds.

For the first time in history, the United States' legacy was visibly infused with a gripping duality in power and justice. After defeating Republican party candidates in the November elections, Vice President Joe Biden and Senator Kamala Harris assumed the highest offices in our esteemed country. Being the first African American, Asian American, and female vice president in the nation, this Howard University graduate, Kamala Harris, was now the second in command. Biden dispelled the impediments associated with ageism. He was now our commander-in-chief. Now, groups marginalized according to their race, age, and background witnessed improbable outcomes disintegrate with each cast ballot. Thus, successfully cracking the racist, sexist, and ageist barriers to entry. But how did such a historic anomaly launch a catalytic change for everyday citizens? That, indeed, is the question to ask.

Although the Biden and Harris ticket secured more votes than any former presidential candidate, the country remained far from united. Those who voted blue down the ballot rejoiced, holding tight to some glimmer of hope. On the contrary, these governmental power changes also widened the divide, magnifying remnants of hate, biases, and ignorance. Measures to re-engage a substantial degree of unity after a tumultuous election season, such as officially marking Juneteenth — a commemorative day crystallizing the eradication of slavery — the moment was short-lived. To make matters worse, media outlets flooded households with the unlawful killings of unarmed Black people, such as George Floyd and Breonna Taylor. Freedom fighters and justice carriers took to the streets to permanently alter these injustice threads pinned into the American legacy. Nationwide protests erupted in a massive attempt to eradicate the guilty-until-proven-innocent narrative all too common for people of color. Unfortunately, to be seen and heard via an equitable lens, occasional drastic measures must be taken, specifically to right the wrongs of the past.

As the Black Lives Matter Movement picked up steam, a nationwide charge to remove public monuments of Confederate leaders resounded across all fifty states, even garnering global support. Hundreds of statues symbolizing the southern states' revolt against the US government during the Civil War stood tall. A modern form of this uprising would be in 2021 when an angry mob of violent protesters entered the US Capitol building, interrupting the Electoral College votes. Sure, it is on a smaller scale, but each individual, in uniform or not, clung to their immutable legacy views and exercised violence. Fast forward, these statues and unethical behaviors unmasked deeper racial oppression. Yet, persistent organizers strongly declined to meekly turn the other cheek.

On the evening of June 29, 2020, my legacy as Chairperson and CEO of Rockdale County hung in the balance of these tense times. Previously, my colleagues and I discussed citizens' interest in removing our Confederate statue. Since the statue was not physically paying a mortgage or sending a kid to college, I tabled the conversation to a later date. We had more pressing issues hanging over our heads, which required immediate attention. Every dollar spent was earmarked for combatting the cyclical effects of the COVID-19 pandemic, such as keeping businesses open and households fed. Yet as major territories, from New York City to Atlanta, were going up in flames, images of the Civil Rights Movement pierced my memory. A few leaders like John Lewis, who was re-elected sixteen times and served as the Georgia Congressional Delegation leader, stood on the right side of history and sparked good trouble. Then, a disturbing call interrupted this contentious flashback.

An anonymous caller said, "Mr. Chairman, we are going to set Conyers afire, if y'all don't get that damn statue down. All the shops in Old Town are going up in smoke, along with the courthouse. Move it or we are coming to your city next."

As calmly as I could manage, I replied, "I understand your concerns. I will discuss this with my team."

Right after that alarming call, I shared this unnerving dilemma with one person, Jay Grover. He asked, rubbing his head, "Well, Oz, what are you going to do?"

"That is why I am talking to you. I need some real advice on this one," I responded.

Until then, Jay and I had weighed the pros and cons of important topics. This process helped me land a sound solution.

"This is a tough one right here. This thing can go either way. If you do decide to remove it, it will be the way you do it," he replied.

When we wrapped up that emergency come-to-Jesus moment, the weight of Rockdale County's and my legacy were planted on my back like a seven-ton African elephant. Any effort to get a minute of shuteye and clear my consciousness exposed contrasting outcomes. I tussled in search of a definitive resolve from my arsenal. The only certainty I arrived upon was that I had to do something and do it fast.

The following morning, I called an emergency meeting with my reliable team. The legacy-altering verdict was delivered.

On the evening of June 29, 2020, I made an executive decision to remove the Confederate statue that had stood in front of Rockdale County's courthouse for 107 years. It would be done in an orderly, communal fashion, just as I described to Jay. Before the public ceremony commenced, eight discontented people locked their arms and positioned themselves around the statue. From their lens, the only way the statue was coming down was if they took them along with it. Of course, the sheriff's department and police team prevented this unnecessary altercation. They de-escalated that situation to a non-violent nature. I released a sigh of relief, continuing the program as planned.

A few hours after nightfall, around ten o'clock, the streets were lined with over twelve hundred people; half supported the removal, and the other half detested the removal. Both groups were ready to go to blows. To combat this brewing tension, the sound counsel of local clergy, including personally invited Black, white, and Hispanic pastors, arrested the atmosphere. Each leader approached the podium and championed a common cause of urgent unity backed by prayer. Heated arguments ceased. Unnerving tensions lessened.

Then, I took the podium, "Tonight, some of you will be happy. Some of you will be mad, but Rockdale County will be a better place in the long run for making that decision," I firmly proclaimed. I held fast to my declaration. Now was not the time to show any weakness.

While the experienced crane company approached the statue and removed it with dignity, I looked out into the crowd. Faces flushed with contrasting emotion. I understood both sides, the reminder that history is not always warm and fuzzy. Yet symbols of unmerited oppression should not stand erect at any courthouse's forefront. I removed my own emotions and operated in the best interest of Rockdale. As the top-ranking government official, I fought like hell to ensure my county was known for something positive. I stand by my decision to this day.

A publicly displayed figure without life can sometimes convey a subliminal message that impedes progress and increases the divide among diverse groups. But by removing these constructs, long-awaited space opens for people to ignite conversations and work collectively. Therefore, coming together and building something positive collectively is facilitated. Ironically, although I was not expecting any standing ovation, a dozen white folks reached out to me. Each citizen expressed gratitude for my bold decision. They did not want their names divulged but stood behind me 100%. People know my heart and true character. I am certain it was the best move. I am proud of my resolution, as well as this country. This act garnered an increased level of trusted leadership and growth for all parties.

Legacy is the vision leaders cast for others to see past their trials and proceed toward glory. It goes beyond the here and now, extending far beyond a single decision or person. Legacy is the cumulative manifestation of the greater good the Lord calls His people to fulfill.

Whether moving from survivor's mode to abundant living or good to better in specific areas, the progressive road can prove to be quite bumpy. I hit speed bumps and took some detours. These interruptions forced me to slow down, smell the roses, and assess my priorities. Ultimately, I arrived at my predestined position with my reputation and faith intact. When you are on the precipice of an amazing breakthrough, tests will emerge, forcing you to stay on the same path or work toward a better one.

Never succumb to the unvalidated opinions of others, but boldly subscribe to the promises of our Creator. Constant battles and trials are inevitable. But remember, your purpose-driven legacy is immutable. Second to God, mentors are optimal copilots as you scale personal and corporate ladders. Such wise advisors offer timely advice as you pinpoint a winning blueprint.

Allow your legacy to set a tone of unity. Love must overpower hate. To that same light, may my former foes now be faithful friends. Fortunately, God surrounds me with "good people." Such treasured individuals believe in my potential and help me construct a global footprint. From Richmond to Rockdale County and multiple road markers in between, my amassed network has been nothing short of amazing. Never forget this golden commandment: do unto others what you would like them to do to you. Walking under this provision helps you weather the storms and make it a new day. Be encouraged. Speak life into yourself.

To God be the glory in all we say and do that brings His will and kingdom to Earth. As the great Martin Luther King Jr. proclaimed: "I have a dream that my four little children will one day live in a nation where they will not be judged by the color of their skin but by the content of their character." That is a legacy, my friend, one of passion, vision, and persistence. What will your legacy be? What garden will you plant and water for future generations?

See you at the top! Our legacies are only going up from here!

Oz

#teamoz

NOTES

NOTES

NOTES

NOTES

NOTES